ROMANCE
Begins in
the KITCHEN

ROMANCE
Begins in
the KITCHEN

ROMANTIC
ITALIAN RECIPES
AND THEIR
COMPLEMENTARY
WINES

Dawn Bause, Modesta DeVita
and Nidal Zaher

Bause House Publications
Commerce Township, Michigan

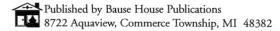Published by Bause House Publications
8722 Aquaview, Commerce Township, MI 48382

Publisher's Cataloging-in-Publication Data
Bause, Dawn.
     Romance begins in the kitchen : romantic Italian recipes and their com-
     plementary wines / by Dawn Bause, Modesta DeVita, and Nidal Zaher.—
     Commerce Twp., MI : Bause House Pub., 1998.
          p.   ill.   cm.
     Includes bibliographical references and index.
     ISBN: 1-9656889-0-9
     1. Cookery, Italian. I. DeVita, Modesta. II. Zaher, Nidal. III. Title.
     TX723 .B38   1997   97-70185
     641.5945—dc21   CIP
Editor: Cassandra M. Withers
Illustrator: Terri Christie

PROJECT COORDINATION BY JENKINS GROUP, INC.

01   00   99   ❖   5   4   3   2   1

Printed in the United States of America

THIS BOOK IS DEDICATED TO FRED W. BAUSE. HIS
LOVE AND APPRECIATION OF FOOD,
WINE AND ROMANCE INSPIRED THIS BOOK AND
HELPED MAKE IT A REALITY.

A SPECIAL THANKS TO CASSANDRA WITHERS
FOR HER LOVE, ENCOURAGEMENT,
AND EDITORIAL ASSISTANCE.

Contents

The Menus...8

Introduction by Dawn Bause.......................9

Meet Modesta DeVita................................11

Meet Nidal Zaher.....................................12

Acknowledgments 13

Romantic Dinners for Two.......................17

It All Starts in the Kitchen 19

Setting the Table...................................21

Stocking the Pantry................................25

Italian Cooking Secrets 27

A Modern Approach to Food & Wine Pairing ..29

The Menus, Wine Lists and Recipes....................37

Wine Glossary 165

Bibliography 169

Index...171

Additional Information 173

The Menus

Zucchini Cakes
Ricotta Gnocchi Bolognese
Chicken Saltimbocca
Fresh Berries with Frozen Yogurt
PAGE 37

Seafood Fritters
Spaghettini with Tuna
Veal Scaloppini with Fresh Sage
Bite Size Cream Puffs
PAGE 49

Pizza Capricciosa
Ricotta Agnolotti
Seared Salmon
Tiramisù
PAGE 59

Caeser Salad
Pasta with Zucchini
and Shitake Mushrooms
Grilled Lamb Chops
Stuffed Apple Wrapped in Phyllo
PAGE 69

Anchovy and
Black Olive Crostini
Seafood Ravioli with
Red Pepper Sauce
Veal Milanese
Macedonia
PAGE 79

Mozzarella Balls with Pesto
Vegetable Lasagna
Chicken Breasts with Rosemary
Zuccotto alla Ricotta
PAGE 91

Stuffed Eggplant Roll-Ups
Spaghettini Marinara
Tilapia Pizzaiola
Norma's Cannoli
PAGE 103

Fried Baby Artichokes
Seafood Pasta
Grilled Veal Chops
Espresso Granita
PAGE 115

Bruschetta with Roasted Peppers
Spaghetti and Meatballs
Chicken Florentine
Italian Kisses
PAGE 125

Portobello Napolean
Fresh Vegetable Pasta
Grilled Shrimp
Grilled Banana and Pineapple
PAGE 135

Crab Meat Crostini
Cannelloni Stuffed with Shrimp
Veal Scaloppini with Artichokes
and Sundried Tomatoes
Apple Sachets
PAGE 145

Caprese Salad
Asparagus Risotto
Chicken Parmesan
Italian Waffle Baskets
PAGE 155

Introduction

WHEN I GOT MARRIED I PROMISED MYSELF I would do everything I could to keep that euphoric, almost indescribable feeling of being "in love" alive in my marriage. I vowed I would remain open to learning, and would never stop looking for new ways to add excitement and spice to our daily lives.

Soon I learned one of the easiest and most effective ways to keep that romantic fire burning was to master the fine art of "dining-in". Today, many years later, my husband still rushes home to me, a glass of wine, and the good smells coming from the kitchen. My kitchen has become a place where I confirm my love for life, my husband, my family and friends. Cooking fulfills a basic human need to bring pleasure to others and to give of oneself.

Romance Begins in the Kitchen offers wonderful ideas for preparing, and presenting elegant and enjoyable home-cooked meals for two. We have made your work easier by planning the menus, selecting the wines, and organizing the recipes. There are suggestions for creating an "enchanting atmosphere" in the kitchen and at the table. Plus, we will show you how to initiate "a little romance" during those special times you decide to "dine-in" with your loved one.

We have selected Italian country recipes because the Italian way of cooking and preparing food comes from the heart. Modesta DeVita, born and raised in Italy, has selected delicious family recipes that are healthy and uncomplicated. Her recipes center around fresh vegetables, herbs, fish, poultry and pasta!

The wine suggestions for our menus came about because of an ever-growing interest in food and wine matching. Nidal's classes on the subject have tripled in the past several years. His chapter entitled "A Modern Approach to Food & Wine Pairing" is a not only a simple and fun introduction to the art of food and wine matching but is also very interesting and informative.

There is no question that the presentation and serving of food and wine is one of the most loving gestures one human being can offer to another. We have evidence supporting our declarations that love can be ignited, nurtured and even rekindled with the simple offering of a home-cooked meal or two!

The positives of taking the time to prepare a romantic home-cooked meal far outweigh the negatives. And, so I ask, are you ready to move on to the kitchen? As they say in Italy... "Andiamo!"

Dawn Bause

Meet Modesta De Vita

IF YOU SHOULD FIND YOURSELF IN A CONVERSATION about exceptional Italian cuisine, undoubtedly the name MODESTA DEVITA will be mentioned. She is a co-creator and one of the original owners of the highly acclaimed "Ristorante di Modesta." Her homemade vegetable lasagna, seafood ravioli with roasted red pepper sauce, thin crust pizzas, crab meat crostini, homemade cannoli, and Tiramisù are just a few of the specialties Modesta shares with us in this cookbook.

Modesta's love for food began in her native homeland of Italy. Although she was born and raised in Rome, ancient family cooking secrets have been passed down for generations from her ancestors who originated in the region of Abruzzi. Many of Italy's best chefs have come from this area which is well known for its superb gastronomic specialties.

Today Modesta continues to work her magic as a food consultant for many of the most elegant and discriminating party planners. She also shares her knowledge of the fine art of ancient Italian cuisine with students and food connoisseurs who attend her cooking classes, seminars and demonstrations.

Modesta demonstrates the art of combining dishes harmoniously to create twelve unforgettable menus and their corresponding recipes. Have fun and *Buon Appetito!*

Meet Nidal Zaher

Nidal Zaher, is a certified sommelier, and has over ten years of successful working experience in the wine industry-encompassing fine dining restaurants and retail. He has served as the Wine Director of the Detroit International Wine Auction for several years – the largest charity wine auction outside of the California wine country. Nidal has recently culminated his career by establishing "Sommelier Connections", a wine consulting company that is dedicated to enhancing the appreciation of wine. He teaches wine classes, conducts wine seminars and tastings, and consults with restaurants about setting up wine lists and developing staff training programs. He also appraises wine cellars, and is a noted cellar planner and designer. Nidal was inducted into the prestigious Chaîne des Rôtisseurs, an International Gastronomic Association dedicated to promoting the culinary arts and preserving the camaraderie and pleasures of the table. Nidal takes us on a journey around the world with his wine selections for our menus. He insists that the final stop on the wine odyssey... is the dinner table. Nothing brings out the best in both the food and the wine better than successfully combining the two.

Nidal's formula for matching food and wine is innovative, simple and fun. He believes it is an art that every one of us can learn. In his chapter entitled "A Modern Approach to Food & Wine Pairing" Nidal gives us some basic principles for mastering "the art of eating and drinking well."

Acknowledgments

WE WISH TO THANK all those people who have contirbuted so much to the making of this book: Diane Welage, Suzanne Helms-Yanok, Jill Melkonian, Assunta DeVita, Italo DeVita, Lisa Santori-Peralta, Yiannis Karimalis, Monica Leseman, Paula Wasilewski, Marc Jonna of The Merchant of Vino, Ron Cirone, David Gardner, Greg Raft of Zypher Design Works, Alex Moore and Barbara Hodge of The Jenkins Group, Wayne Carter, Carla Akan, Malek Taha, Dianne Hemme, Jenine Sassak, Cara Withers, Kay Masuda, Dorian DeVita, Del Reddy, Sue Macros, Barbaro Grundell, Ginny Tomlinson, Johnna Sassak, Henrietta Gardner, Nicole Anderson, Luigi Cattelan, Dino Santori, Dick Masuda, Josephine Pacifici, Pat Karimalis, Daniela Roher, Giovanna Bitonte, Angie Kaufman, Susan Carlow, Dianne Farkas.

ROMANCE
Begins in
the KITCHEN

ROMANTIC DINNERS FOR TWO

IF YOU'RE SINGLE, RECENTLY MARRIED, married with children but can send them to a friend or neighbor for the night, or if your family has grown and you're a twosome once again... this book is for you. Cooking and creating meals that excite the appetite, and nourish the body and the soul, is easier than you ever thought possible.

When it's just the two of you, you can afford to splurge on wines, fresh flowers, premium produce, imported cheeses, fresh baked breads, and the freshest seafood, poultry and meats making these dinners all the more wonderful.

One way to make "cooking for two" an adventure in love is to make some of the recipes with your mate or lover. Today, both men and women are quite competent in the kitchen, and enjoy cooking, so don't be foolish, encourage teamwork! You will discover that just about everything in the kitchen is easier to do when you are two. Divide up the work and you'll both enjoy dinner even more. Plus hours spent together in the kitchen will do wonders for strengthening the bonds of love, and the closeness that come from a shared experience.

Okay, so what if your lover is not interested in cooking? Well, then he or she can always help grocery shop, unload the groceries, set the table, or help cleanup. Remind them of the closeness that comes from a shared experience!

And if you really want this to be a pleasurable experience, then don't forget the kisses, love pats, words of praise, and passionate embraces in the kitchen, at the table and beyond. *Viva l'amore!*

$\mathcal{I}$T ALL STARTS IN THE KITCHEN

$\mathcal{T}$HE KITCHEN... IT'S A MAGICAL WORD, and a magical place in the home. Of all the rooms, the kitchen can feed the soul and warm a heart. According to recent research we spend as much as 60 percent of our time in the kitchen. We not only prepare meals and eat there, we also read, write our bills, make phone calls and entertain family and friends in and around the kitchen. The kitchen truly is the heart of a home and a great place to express your creativity, your love of life, and your own personality.

Creating an "atmosphere of enchantment"

Let's look at some old and new ideas for creating an inviting atmosphere of beauty and efficiency in your kitchen. Whether your kitchen is large or small, old or new, it' a room that should always be evolving. Like people, a room becomes boring and old if it never changes.

There are many subtle and elegant ways you can rearrange and reorganize "things" in your kitchen. We know you can't move the refrigerator, stove, sink, counters or cabinets, unless you're willing to do some major remodeling, but you can change or rearrange everything else. Your objective is to have your things organized, handy and attractively displayed.

Begin by cleaning out, and reorganizing all the cupboards and drawers. Then clear everything off the counter tops except for those small appliances you use "everyday". This gives you more working space and areas for you to create beautiful still lifes with plants, fruits, vegetables, bowls, baskets, bottles and art objects. If just the thought of tackling this job makes you feel overwhelmed, think of engaging the services of a professional organizer, or a friend or family member. Remember, "everything in the kitchen is easier when you are two."

Once the kitchen is cleaned and organized, it's time to start adding some personal touches. Accessories and decorative accents add personality, warmth, beauty and charm. Here is a list of some ideas:

- Potted plants, topiaries, flowers, and herbs. Keep the plants clean and healthy. Move or give away plants that look tired or need a little T.L.C.

- Dried flowers and herbs tied with raffia or beautiful ribbons will also add beauty. When they become faded and dusty discard and start with something new.

- Hang various shape baskets, gleaming brass and copper utensils and molds from ceiling hooks or on the wall for decoration when not in use.

- Decorate walls with lithographs and paintings, hand painted ceramic plates and bowls.

- Mirrors are great in the kitchen. If you have a wall space above your counter back splash, install a mirror that fills the whole space from the back splash to the cabinets. It adds sparkle and space to your kitchen.

- Use creative lighting and fixtures above the sink, under the counters and over the kitchen table.

- Imported hand-painted Italian, French or Spanish tiles also make great borders and designs on your walls. There are also gorgeous stencils you can paint on.

- Find an antique or unusual wine rack to store all those bottles of wonderful new wines you're going to learn about in this book. Start a corkscrew collection.

- Wooden spoons displayed in a beautiful crock. Collect them from your travels around the world.

- Display unusual decanters filled with different oils, vinegars and herbs.

- Several times a year replace and update your potholders and dish towels.

- Collect and wear beautiful aprons while in the kitchen.

- Use an antique dresser, baker's cabinet or French armoire in the kitchen to store silverware, dishes and linens.

- Keep your refrigerator clean and organized. Use see-through containers for juices and milk, clear bowls for fruits and vegetables. Store eggs in an antique wire basket.

- For a beautiful surprise place a small vase of fresh flowers in the refrigerator. You'll be amazed how long they last and how fun it is to see them each time you open the refrigerator door.

SETTING THE TABLE

IF THE KITCHEN IS THE HEART OF THE HOME, the dinner table is the heart of your family life. Setting a pretty table determines the tone and mood for a meal. It will powerfully convey affection, warmth and thoughtfulness long before the first appetizer is served. Architect Frank Lloyd Wright is quoted as saying, "Dining is and always was a great artistic opportunity." We suggest you take advantage of this chance to be creative by setting a beautiful table.

Start by bringing out your prettiest dishes, crystal glasses, silverware, linens, vases, candlesticks, collectibles and unusual accessories. Add additional excitement by mixing patterns, colors and styles. Note, if you don't have fine china, crystal, linens and silver then we suggest you start collecting these items at antique fairs or garage sales. We're only talking about place settings for two, and since you can mix and match, it'll be easy and fun acquiring these special pieces. Remember that variety is the spice of life!

Think of the table as your stage, and you are the set designer. Your goal is to turn your dinner table into a visual fantasy. After the table linens, plates, glasses and silverware have been put in place, it's time to add the finishing touches.

In the dim light of candles

The world gets smaller and more intimate when you are seated at the dinner table lit only by candles. Only your lover's face and the food in front of you are visible. It's as though the rest of the world has faded away for this special moment in time. The flickering of the flames cast a magical glow on your faces and a warm, peaceful feeling in your hearts. Candles are the single most romantic prop. It's never too late to start a candlestick collection. Crystal candlesticks in various sizes and shapes all grouped together make a marvelous display of light. Silver or brass candelabras have an elegant and extravagant feel to them. Small votives grouped or scattered around the table are gorgeous. Or you can float small tea candles in a bowl, or in wine or champagne glasses filled with water. Once again be creative. Look in magazines and books for ideas.

Flower power

Fresh flowers add color and excitement to any table. The towering formal centerpieces of yesteryear that obstructed sight lines and isolated guests are a thing of the past. Floral designers have replaced the usual bouquet of flowers with creative conversation pieces. Large bouquets are divided up into small individual arrangements and set around the table or at each place setting to create an atmosphere of intimacy. Fruits, vegetables and unusual accessories are mixed with flowers to surprise and delight. Here are a few creative ideas:

- Try using small dainty flowers nestled in wine glasses, teacups, small vases or votives.
- Hollow out the center of a couple artichokes and fill with flowers or small candles.
- Decorate the stems of antique wineglasses with small flower blossoms tied with raffia. Use all the same color flowers. Baby roses, daffodils, or hyacinths buds are a few ideas.
- Fill silver teapots, sugar bowls, and bud vases with tulips, tea roses, or peonies.
- Intertwine variegated ivy and flowers to form napkin rings. Try using a single rose or fresh lilacs. You can also use a sprig of fresh rosemary to make the ring.
- A spectacular way to keep a bottle of white wine or sparkling mineral water chilled at the table is with a icy flower jacket. To make one, fill an empty milk carton two-thirds full with water. Add flowers or herbs and a bottle containing vodka or aquavit and freeze. (Small roses standing up with their stems are gorgeous!) Remove the carton and the bottle of vodka. Insert your bottle of white wine or water, and place it on your table in a lovely flat bowl to catch the drips.
- Fill small silver boxes or decorative boxes with a little moss, an orchid and other blooms to create a miniature garden at each place setting.
- Place a white gardenia at each place setting
- Decorate the back of each chair with a rose and orchid bouquet tied with a beautiful organza ribbon.
- Between two clear glass plates place some fresh flower petals
- If you insist on a centerpiece, make sure it is not too high. Be creative. Try combining vegetables and fruits with flowers. An example would be mixing purple cabbage, roses, eggplant and turnips. Think about form, color and texture. Incorporate something old or special into the centerpiece to add a personal touch.

Cloth napkins add a gracious touch to any table

Like candles and flowers, cloth napkins make a meal special. Use them whenever possible, not just on special occasions or holidays. Collect them on your travels and at antique stores. Learn the distinguished art of napkin folding and practice it. Listed below are a couple simple folding techniques for you to try.

- Using a large napkin, best size is 24 inches square. Begin by folding the napkin in half to form a triangle. Then bring points to the top of the triangle. Tie a wide ribbon around the middle or you can use a napkin ring.

- Fold the top and bottom edge of napkin towards the center. Pleat the whole napkin the opposite direction from the first folds. Press pleats firmly. Center napkin in a napkin ring and spread pleats into a fan-like shape.

- Fold top and bottom edges of the napkin to the center. Turn the seam side down. Then tie the center of the napkin with ribbons, cording, ivy, flowers, or fresh herbs (a sprig of rosemary looks and smells wonderful) or place in a napkin ring. Turn the napkin vertically on the plate at each place setting.

- Again using a large napkin. Fold the napkin in half diagonally forming a triangle. Fold the bottom of the triangle towards the top point about 2/3 of the way. Then loosely pleat or gather the part you folded up. Tie with a beautiful organza ribbon or cording near the bottom and fan the gathered part out.

Arrangement of plates, glasses and utensils

It's amazing how many of us are still confused about the proper way to set the table. The arrangement of plates, glasses and silverware is fairly standard. Here are the basic rules.

The basic setting should be in place before you sit down to the table.

- The dinner plate or service plate should be in the center with the napkin placed on top of it.

- Glasses are placed above the knives to the right of the plate. There will be a water goblet, and extending to the right, a champagne glass, one or two wine glasses, and a sherry glass (that is if all the above beverages are served.) Otherwise, use only the glasses you will be needing.

- To the left of the plate, place the dessert fork closest to the plate, then a dinner fork to the left of it, a fish fork, if needed, goes to the left of the dinner fork, and a salad fork to the left of it.

- To the right of the plate place the meat knife first (closest to the plate) then the fish knife, if needed, followed by the salad knife. A soup or fruit spoon goes to the right of the knives.

Note: Utensils are used in order from the outside in.

- A butter plate is placed above the forks to the left of the service plate, and the butter knife is set across the butter plate.

Note: Serve plates from the left, and clear them from the right.

Stocking the Pantry

Keeping essential ingredients on hand is the basis for having fun in the kitchen. When the cupboard is bare... beware. To complement the menus in this book, we have compiled a list of staples that you should try to always keep stocked.

Dry Ingredients
- Pasta (some examples are angel hair, spaghetti, farfalle, linguine, and penne)
- Italian Arborio Rice
- Plain breadcrumbs, store-bought or homemade, using stale Italian bread
- Unbleached flour
- Yeast
- Mushrooms (shitake, porcini etc.)
- Espresso
- Cocoa
- Bittersweet Chocolate

Canned or Bottled Ingredients
- Extra virgin olive oil
- Italian plum tomatoes
- Capers
- Anchovies in oil
- Tuna fish in oil
- Vinegar (Balsamic and Red Wine)
- Dijon mustard
- Worcestershire sauce
- Black olives (Kalamata or Greek)

Dried Seasonings
- Red pepper flakes
- Cinnamon sticks
- Whole nutmeg
- Oregano
- Salt
- Black peppercorns

Fresh Seasonings and Produce
- Garlic cloves
- Basil
- Sage
- Rosemary
- Italian Parsley
- Dill
- Lemons
- Carrots
- Celery
- Onions
- Tomatoes
- Hot peppers (red, yellow, jalapeno, habenero)
- Red Peppers (roast store in oil in the fridge)
- Parmigiano Reggiano Cheese
- Fresh mozzarella balls
- Traditional mozzarella cheese for grating
- Ricotta cheese
- Homemade chicken stock (frozen in ice cube trays)

ITALIAN COOKING SECRETS

- Use only fresh herbs. Never use dried basil, parsley, rosemary or sage. They will change the flavor of the dish dramatically.
- When your recipe calls for garlic always use fresh garlic cloves, never use garlic salt or garlic powder. It will give the dish a chemical aftertaste.
- Salt is essential for enhancing the flavor of the food. While too much salt will ruin a dish, too little may defeat it. Add a little at a time and taste your dish frequently.
- Always buy the freshest ingredients possible.
- Use canned plum tomatoes when local vine-ripened tomatoes are not available.
- Never buy chicken broth. Anytime you have chicken you have the base for broth. Stock can begin with a whole chicken or from the skin and bones of a chicken breast that you boned. Freeze homemade chicken stock in ice cube trays.
- Use fresh mozzarella, ricotta and real Parmigiano-Reggiano cheeses when the recipe calls for them.
- Do not overcook sauces. The less you fuss with them the fresher they will taste.
- Salt pasta water after it has started to boil. Never put oil in the water as this coats the pasta and inhibits it from absorbing the sauce properly.
- The most important secret of all is to do everything in your power to make eating together with your loved one a joyous and festive occasion.

A MODERN APPROACH TO FOOD & WINE PAIRING

by Nidal Zaher

What's wrong with today's gourmands, sommeliers and other so-called experts on food and wine? Many times, they are too authoritarian in their presentation, giving recommendations based on old rules.

I also feel the subject matter is so vast, it is almost impossible for any one person to be considered a true food and wine-matching expert. There are more than a million different wine labels and even more varieties of food, spices and herbs. The best any of us so-called experts can do is to offer guidance and make recommendations from our own experience. When all is said and done, the only real expert is you. The best food and wine match is the one that *pleases your palate.*

Food and wine matching can be a lot of fun if it is treated as an art, rather than a science. I believe one has to be adventurous, take chances, and even risk embarrassment, in order to become a truly masterful artist. The exciting part of food and wine matching today is that people are more interested in trying different foods and wines. The results are a wider variety of wines and specialty foods being offered to us by retailers and restaurants.

I want to introduce you to some of the fundamental principles about food and wine matching in this chapter. *(Please note, I have been careful not to call these principles "rules" so that you won't be afraid to break them!)* My objective is for you to learn how to enhance the flavors and pleasures of the food and the wine by serving them together. A basic understanding of how food and wine work together is what helps in achieving a good match. So, let's begin.

In describing the wine criteria for certain food matches, I have tried to be scientific, accurate, and most of all, objective. In doing so, some of the terms I have used may be difficult to understand, so please refer to the glossary for clarification when necessary.

As you experiment with food and wine, you will notice certain patterns in which wine and food matches can be good, ordinary or poor. Look for the following patterns:

1. **<u>Synergism:</u>** The most charismatic action of food and wine working together. This action

occurs when food and wine combine to create an aftertaste that is different from the after-taste of the two consumed individually. Most often this aftertaste takes the form of a third flavor that is not found in either the food or the wine. The third flavor can be perceived as good or bad. For example, Port wine and Roquefort cheese together create a pleasant impression of butterscotch or vanilla in the mouth. This flavor can't be experienced when the Port or Rocquefort are tasted separately. On the contrary, a tannic red wine consumed with anchovies can create a completely unpleasant third flavor that is described as metallic.

2. **Refreshment:** In this pattern the wine is usually a refreshment to the food more often than the two are refreshing to each other. An example of this would be eating salty roasted almonds while sipping a cold glass of white Zinfandel. This combination would create an exuberant feeling, as the wine would offer the cool relief of thirst. In this case, the wine is the refreshing element. A good match such as a dry Sherry with the salty roasted almonds can enhance the nutty flavors in both the Sherry and the almonds, thus the food and the wine are refreshing to each other.

3. **Neutrality:** Happens when neither the food nor the wine turns more acidic, harsher, bitter or sweeter. The food and wine go their own way without affecting one another. While neutrality doesn't sound very attractive, it is a great improvement over various matches that produce unpleasant additional tastes.

4. **Transformation:** Results when either the food or the wine remains unchanged, while the other appears completely different. For example, consider first the complexity, finesse, and great concentration of Château Margaux, an expensive red from the Bordeaux region in France. A good way to ruin this wine is matching it with artichoke hearts, making the wine taste thin, acidic, and sweet. The wine, in this case, is transformed, but there is no change in the flavor of the artichoke hearts themselves.

Achieving a Good Match

Matching food and wine is like forging a relationship. As with most relationships, they can be happy or not, and may work for different reasons. Many of these matches may seem irrational. Having said that, let us continue.

A food and wine match can be achieved either *by analogy* or *by contrast. Analogy* means the food and the wine are strikingly similar in some way. Examples: sweet and sweet, rich and rich. *Contrast* means the food and wine are strikingly different in some way. Examples: salty and sweet, rich and light.

There are three categories that describe how food and wine can be similar or different.
- Components
- Flavors
- Textures

Matching Food and Wine by Components

The first and easiest way to match food and wine is by matching the components. Components are the basic food and wine elements that correspond to the five sensory perceptions on the tongue, i.e. sweetness, acidity or sourness, saltiness, and bitterness.

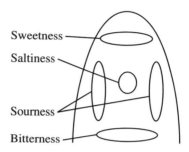

Note: Although matching by components is not as challenging, it is the basic components in food and wine that determines the success of the match.

Defining Components

A. **Sweetness:** Food sweetness comes from natural sugar, or the addition of sugar. Wine sweetness comes from the natural sugar in the grapes.

B. **Sourness:** Food sourness comes from high levels of acidity, whether natural as in lemons, or added as in salad dressing. Wine sourness comes from a naturally occurring high level of acidity.

C. **Saltiness:** Food saltiness comes from natural salt as in briny oysters, or from the addition of salt. Wine does not frequently offer salty flavors, though some wines like Manzanilla Sherry, are described as having a salty tang.

D. **Bitterness:** Food bitterness is occasionally found, but it's rarely a pleasant perception, as in Belgian endive or eggplant. Wine bitterness is usually a turn off, as well. Often wine bitterness is the result of too much tannin from fermenting the wine with the stems, seeds, and skin. It can also be caused from too much wood from fermenting or aging the wine in oak barrels.

Guidelines to Keep in Mind When Considering Component Matches:

1. Avoid matching food with high acidity with a wine with low acidity as the food can wash out the low acid wine. Example: a ripe tomato salad in a vinaigrette dressing and white Rhône wine.

2. When matching food and wine based on contrasting components of salty food and acidic wine, select a wine that does not have high alcohol content as the wine would taste bitter. Example: salty potato chips and a young Riesling from Alsace.

3. When matching sweet wines and sweet food, it is best if the wine is sweeter than the food. Example: Demi-Sec Champagne and a light fruit tart.

Examples of Food and Wine Matches Based on Components

	Food	(Component)	Wine	(Component)
Contrasting:	Raw Oysters	(Salty)	Muscadet	(Acidic)
	Rocquefort or Blue Cheese	(Salty)	Sauternes	(Sweet)
Similar:	Fruit Tart	(Sweet)	Demi-Sec Champagne	(Sweet)
	Crème Brulée	(Sweet)	Sauternes	(Sweet)

Matching Food and Wine by Flavors

With flavor matches you can be much more creative and adventurous than with component matches. Flavor matches are a little trickier, and although it is easier to make a bad match, flavor matching through experimentation, risk taking, and rule breaking can produce the greatest food and wine matches.

Defining Flavors

Flavors are elements of food and wine that are perceived by the olfactory nerve as fruity, minty, herbal, nutty, flowery, et cetera. Flavor is the range of complex tastes that give distinction to all foods and wines. What we generally describe as flavor is actually something we smell. Once our tongue has perceived the basic elements in the food and wine, the olfactory nerve takes over.

Remember our tongue cannot pick up fruity or minty flavors. It's the interaction of the nose and the palate that enables us to find those specific flavors.

Guidelines to Keep in Mind When Considering Flavor Matches

1. Use caution when it comes to flavor similarity and avoid generalities whenever possible. If you find a food and a wine that really do have similar flavors, look for a specific flavor. For example: Almonds and Fino Sherry (nutty and nutty) will usually go well together.

2. For flavor contrasts you must use your own judgement and personal preferences. A few examples of great contrasts in flavor would be: Catfish and Pouilly Fumé (fishy and herbal) or smoked ham and German Riesling (smoky and flowery) or prime rib and aged red Burgundy (meaty and earthy).

3. Keep in mind that some foods can only take contrasts never similarities. For example, you can't find a fish, lamb or garlic flavored wine, but the addition of herbs, fruits, nuts, etc. to a fish, lamb or garlic dish will help create flavor similarity with the wine, if that's what you want to do.

Please note that the above guidelines are not meant to be rigid rules. They are suggestions offered only to make you sensitive to the nuances involved in matching flavors.

Examples of Matching Food and Wine by Flavors

	Food	(Flavor)	Wine	(Flavor)
Contrasting:	Parmigiano Reggiano	(Cheesy)	Young Italian Red ex. Valpolicella	(Fruity)
	Smoked Ham	(Smoky)	Dry Riesling	(Flowery)
Similar:	Grilled Leg of Lamb with Rosemary	(Herbal)	Cabernet Sauvignon	(Herbal)
	Roasted Almonds	(Nutty)	Fino Sherry	(Nutty)
	Raw Oysters	(Mineraly)	Chablis	(Mineraly)

Matching Food and Wine by Textures

Texture matches are probably the most stimulating, since your entire oral cavity is involved in sensing textures. Component matches, on the other hand, involve only the tongue, while flavor matches involve mostly the nose.

Defining Textures

Textures are those qualities in food and wine that we feel in the mouth. Examples are: softness, smoothness, roundness, richness, thickness, thinness, creaminess, chewiness, oiliness, harshness or silkiness. Texture also indicates those qualities in food and wine that correspond to sensations of touch and temperature, such as spiciness.

Guidelines to Keep in Mind When Considering Texture Matches

1. Beware of a double whammy when matching similar textured items. Some matches can be ruined by too much of a good thing; such as matching a gooey dessert and a highly viscous dessert wine.

2. Contrasting textures with a food that is too rich for the wine, or a wine that is too rich for the food, is not a good match either. Examples: chunky lamb stew, with a light red Burgundy, or a big style Barolo overwhelming a lightly sautéed veal scaloppini.

Examples of Matching Food and Wine by Texture

	Food	(Texture)	Wine	(Texture)
Contrasting:	Flourless Pear Soufflé	(Light)	Muscat de Beaumes -de-Venise	(Rich)
Similar	Braised Lamb Shanks	(Rich)	Gigondas	(Rich)
	Black-eyed Peas	(Rich)	Zinfandel, Napa Valley	(Rich)

Once you learn how to decipher food and wine in terms of components, flavors and textures, you'll never be puzzled again by matching the limitless menus of the world with the infinite wine labels of the universe.

With a little practice and experimentation, you'll be able to make excellent food and wine matches. I truly believe your palate can teach you more than any book on food and wine matching. *Here's a toast to that day!*

Note:

The *wine suggestions* listed for the menus in this book are meant to be an educational guide. When preparing a menu for two people it is not always economically feasible to serve a different wine for each course. The symbol of a heart "❤" will appear before some wine selections. This heart indicates a "Romantic Wine Match" that would be appropriate to serve for more than one course. Although, the "Romantic Wine Match" might not match the different courses in the same manner it would for the course I initially recommended. The "Romantic

Wine Match" could be an exhilarating experience allowing you to differentiate between a great match, an average match, and a poor match. After all, life is full of adventures and learning experiences that we should undertake every once in a while!

Price Disclaimer:

Prices listed for the suggested wine lists, are prices I have noted in retail wine stores in the metropolitan Detroit area. No attempt has been made to do an exhaustive survey of prices or to guarantee accuracy. Rather, the prices are listed as an approximate guide. Prices vary depending upon such factors as:

1. **Timing.** Prices will change due to fluctuations in demand, and/or promotional sales on wines.

2. **Dollar value.** The rate of exchange with foreign currencies (only in the case of imported wines.)

3. **Inflation.** Economic factors vary and effect the wine prices accordingly. Since these prices were quoted at the time the book was written, they may very well have increased since that time.

The Menu

Zucchini Cakes
SHREDDED ZUCCHINI, POTATOES AND SAUTÉED ONIONS

Ricotta Gnocchi Bolognese
FRESH RICOTTA DUMPLINGS WITH VEAL MEAT SAUCE

Chicken Saltimbocca
CHICKEN BREASTS SAUTÉED IN GARLIC, WHITE WINE, FRESH SAGE AND
TOPPED WITH PROSCUITTO AND FRESH PARMESAN CHEESE

Fresh Berries with Frozen Yogurt
MARINATED IN GRAND MARNIER

A Little Romance:

Couples fall in love and friendships flourish as a result of quality time spent alone talking to
each other…and what better place to do this than at the dinner table while enjoying a beautifully prepared meal and a glass of wine. Meals are small acts of great importance, and the
rewards are memorable and long lasting. Write and memorize a toast for just the two of you.
Use it whenever you sit down to a meal.

Let's Talk Wines For This Menu

Zucchini Cakes
SHREDDED ZUCCHINI, POTATOES AND SAUTEÉD ONIONS

Wine Criteria:
You can start with a dry sparkling wine from California, Washington State or even Spain.

Suggestions:
Domaine Ste. Michelle Blanc de Blancs Brut, Columbia Valley (Washington State) **$8**
Aria Brut, Catalonia (Spain) **$9**
Domaine Carneros Tattinger Brut, Carneros (California) **$16**
Domaine Chandon Brut, Napa Valley (California) **$12**

or serve a dry Rosé from France
Suggestions:
Domaine Capion Rosé, Rhône Valley (France) **$7**
Syrah Rosé, Rhône Valley (France) **$7**
Sancerre Rosé, Loire Valley (France) **$16**
Tavel Rosé. Rhône Valley (France) **$12**

Ricotta Gnocchi Bolognese
FRESH RICOTTA DUMPLINGS WITH VEAL MEAT SAUCE

Wine Criteria:
Normally ricotta cheese would require a dry unoaked white wine with good acidity, but the dominant ingredient in the dish is the meat sauce. Therefore, it is better to choose a wine that could match the acidity, and the flavor of the sauce. A medium-bodied Chianti Classico, or a medium bodied Cabernet Sauvignon from Sonoma County, California, or Washington State would be spicy with good acidity, as well as a California Sangiovesse.

Suggestions:
Atlas Peak Consenso, Napa Valley (California) **$22**
Beringer "Howell Mountain" Merlot, Napa Valley (California) **$35**
Carneros Creek Fleur de Carneros Pinot Noir, Carneros (California) **$9** *budget choice*
Castello Dei Rampolla Chianti Classico, Tuscany (Italy) **$15**

Chicken Saltimbocca

CHICKEN BREASTS SAUTÉED WITH WHITE WINE, FRESH SAGE,
AND TOPPED WITH PROSCUITTO AND PARMESAN CHEESE

Wine Criteria:
The dominant flavors in the dish would be the proscuitto and the parmesan cheese. So, choose an elegant, oaky, dry Sauvignon Blanc.

Suggestions:
Cloudy Bay Sauvignon Blanc, Marlborough, South Island (New Zealand) **$16**
Pouilly Fumé, Loire Valley (France) **$16**
Murphy-Goode Fumé Blanc, Alexander Valley (California) **$11**
Robert Mondavi Sauvignon Blanc "SLD", Napa Valley (California) **$19**

If you are really out to impress, select an elegant style, oaky dry Chardonnay or a Grand Cru Burgundy.

Suggestions:
Pahlmeyer Chardonnay, Napa Valley (California) **$45**
Batard-Montrachet, Burgundy, (France) **$120-$200**
Talbott Diamont "T" Chardonnay, Napa Valley (California) **$45**
Château Laville Haut Brion, Graves (France) **$55**

Or you can serve a cool climate, medium-bodied red with acidity.

Suggestions:
Valpolicella Superiore, Veneto (Italy) **$7**
Chinon, Loire Valley (France) **$15**
(This wine is produced from the Cabernet Franc Grapes.)

Fresh Berries with Frozen Yogurt
MARINATED IN GRAND MARNIER

Wine Criteria:
If black fruits are used, select a medium-sweet fortified wine, such as California Black Muscat or Sweet Red from Veneto, Italy.

Suggestions:
Quady Elysium, Central Valley (California) **$12 ¹/₂ bt**
Quady Essensia, Central Valley (California) **$12 ¹/₂ bt**
Reicoto Della Valpolicella, Veneto (Italy) **$35**

If you use red berries such as cherries, strawberries, raspberries, you may select a light-bodied dry sparkling wine similar to the style suggested with the zucchini cakes appetizer.

You may also try a botrytized sweet white wine such as young Sauternes or Muscat de Beaumes-du-Venise from the Rhône Valley, France except with raspberries. My personal favorite with raspberries is Brachetto d'Aqui, which is a raspberry infusion sparkling wine.

Zucchini Cakes

Delectable little zucchini and potato pan cakes garnished with a dollop of
fresh sour cream for a mouth-watering appetizer.

1 MEDIUM ZUCCHINI, SHREDDED

1 SMALL POTATO, PEELED AND GRATED

2 TABLESPOONS ONIONS, CHOPPED FINE

1 WHOLE EGG (BEATEN)

2 TABLESPOONS FLOUR

$1/2$ TEASPOON SALT

PEPPER TO TASTE

1 TEASPOON ITALIAN PARSLEY OR DILL, CHOPPED FINE

PINCH RED PEPPER FLAKES

3 TABLESPOONS FRYING OIL (MAZOLA OR CANOLA)

2 TABLESPOONS SOUR CREAM (FOR GARNISH)

Shred zucchini. Let set in a strainer for 1 hour to drain liquid. Peel and grate potatoes. Chop onions fine. Mix zucchini, potato, onion, flour, egg, salt, parsley and hot pepper flakes.

Heat oil in frying pan over medium high heat. Spoon a tablespoon of mixture into hot oil and brown on both sides. Remove from frying pan and place on a paper towel to absorb excess oil.

Garnish: Dollop of sour cream, fresh dill and a kiss!

Ricotta Gnocchi with Meat Sauce

The ricotta used in this recipe makes the gnocchi lighter and more delicate than the traditional potato gnocchi. Served here with a veal meat sauce to add texture and flavor.

Meat Sauce

1 MEDIUM ONION, MINCED

1 CARROT, MINCED

1 STALK CELERY, MINCED

2 CLOVES GARLIC, MINCED

5 LEAVES FRESH BASIL, CHOPPED

1/4 CUP WHITE WINE

1 POUND GROUND VEAL

1 CUP MILK, LOW FAT

2 TABLESPOONS OLIVE OIL

1- 16 OZ. CAN OF PLUM TOMATOES WITH JUICE, CHOPPED

1 TEASPOON SALT

PEPPER TO TASTE

OPTIONAL: PINCH RED PEPPER FLAKES

In a heavy skillet, sauté onions and garlic until golden, add carrots, and celery. Add wine and let evaporate, about 2 minutes. Add meat, stir until cooked through. Add salt and pepper, then add 1/2 cup milk and cook for 10 minutes. Add tomatoes, optional red pepper flakes, and simmer for 1 hour. As the juice cooks down, add remainder of milk a little at a time. Remember this is suppose to be a thicker sauce.

Ricotta Gnocchi

1 CUP RICOTTA CHEESE, DRAINED IF NECESSARY

1 CUP FLOUR, PLUS EXTRA FOR WORKING SURFACE

1 LARGE EGG, BEATEN

4 TABLESPOONS PARMIGIANO-REGGIANO* OR PARMESAN, FRESHLY GRATED

DASH NUTMEG FRESHLY GRATED

1 TEASPOON SALT

2 SPRIGS ITALIAN PARSLEY (FOR GARNISH)

3 QUARTS WATER FOR COOKING GNOCCHI

1 TEASPOON SALT

* *Parmigiano-Reggiano made only in Italy under the strictest legal and technical supervision. It is considered the only real parmesan. Although it is a little harder to find and a little more expensive… the taste, consistency and cooking qualities make it worth the money spent. To tell whether you are buying real parmesan, look for cheese that has a dark golden rind stamped with the words "Parmigiano Reggiano."*

Drain ricotta in a colander if using fresh. On a wood cutting board, or large working surface, place ricotta. Make a well in the middle and add the egg, salt, nutmeg, 2 tablespoons parmesan cheese and flour. Gently fold dough with a spatula until it is firm but not sticky, and you are able to form a ball. If dough is too sticky, add 1 tablespoon flour at a time until it is workable.

In a medium saucepan, bring 2 cups of water to a boil in order to test several of your gnocchi to make sure they are not too soft and will stay together before you proceed. Salt boiling water. Take a spoonful of dough and roll it into an oval ball, drop it in the boiling water and let cook until it floats. If it stays together then proceed. (If they are too soft and fall apart in the boiling water, add a little more flour to the dough before proceeding.)

Divide dough into quarters and roll out on a floured board until it resembles a thick sausage shaped roll 2-3" thick. Cut roll in half and roll each piece out again (flour hands if necessary) until they resemble a long bread stick, 3/4" thick. Then cut into 1 inch pieces.

With a floured finger, make a dimple in the center of each piece, rolling the gnocchi towards you. The reason for the dimple is to absorb more of the sauce. The gnocchi can be refrigerated on a lightly floured baking sheet for several hours before boiling and serving.

Fill a medium pot with several quarts of water, bring to boil and add salt. Carefully drop ricotta gnocchi into the boiling water one by one. Boil gently until they float. Carefully remove the gnocchi with a slotted spoon.

Return gnocchi to the pan and gently toss with some of the meat sauce. Let stand for 5 minutes. Dish up on individual plates, add a little more sauce and garnish.

Garnish: Freshly grated Parmigiano-Reggiano/parmesan and a sprig of parsley.

Diagram #1

 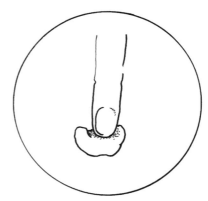

Chicken Saltimbocca

Tender, succulent chicken breasts sautéed in white wine, fresh sage and topped with mozzarella, prosciutto and fresh parmesan. The secret to this dish besides it's wonderful flavoring, is the way the meat is sliced very thin, and then pounded to an even thinner dimension. Sometimes pounded as thin as $\frac{1}{8}$ to $\frac{1}{16}$ of an inch. The thinness is what contributes to the delicacy of the finished dish.

2 WHOLE CHICKEN BREASTS (BONED AND SKINLESS)

3 TABLESPOONS FLOUR

$\frac{1}{4}$ CUP DRY WHITE WINE

1 CLOVE GARLIC

3 TABLESPOONS OLIVE OIL

SALT AND PEPPER TO TASTE

8 LEAVES FRESH SAGE*

4 SLICES PROSCIUTTO, SLICED THIN

$\frac{1}{2}$ CUP CHICKEN STOCK

4 SLICES MOZZARELLA CHEESE THINLY SLICED IN TRIANGLE SHAPE

FRESHLY GRATED PARMESAN CHEESE/ PARMIGIANO-REGGIANO SHAVINGS FOR GARNISH

* You can not substitute ground or powdered sage for fresh sage leaves. The flavor will be destroyed.

Cut chicken breasts in half. Place each breast between 2 layers of plastic wrap and pound thin with the flat side of a meat cleaver. (If the breasts are too thick, try slicing them in half horizontally and then pounding them even thinner.) *The proper pounding procedure is to bring the pounder down on the center of the meat and slide from the center outward in one continuous motion. Do this until each chicken breast is thinned out evenly.* Salt and pepper both sides of the chicken and dust generously with flour.

Heat oil and garlic in a large frying pan over medium high heat until hot. Remove the garlic after it is golden. Raise heat to high and sauté the chicken breasts in the hot oil until golden brown on both sides. Add white wine and simmer until it has evaporated. Then add half (¹/₄ cup) of the chicken stock and the fresh sage.

Place a slice of prosciutto and a slice of mozzarella on top of each breast, cover and let simmer for about 5 minutes. Remove from pan, keep warm. De-glaze the pan with the remainder of the chicken stock. Pour over chicken and serve immediately.

Garnish: Fresh shavings of parmesan cheese and fresh sage.

Diagram #2

Fresh Berries with Frozen Yogurt

A simple fruit dish is promoted to an elegant dessert status
with the addition of Grand Marnier.

1 CUP FRESH BERRIES, TRY STRAWBERRIES,

BLUEBERRIES, RASPBERRIES, AND BLACKBERRIES*

1/4 CUP SPARKLING WINE OR CHAMPAGNE

3 TABLESPOONS GRAND MARNIER

1 TABLESPOON SUGAR

2 FRESH MINT SPRIGS

2 SCOOPS VANILLA FROZEN YOGURT

• *If any of these berries are not available select those that are in season and look good.*

Rinse berries in sparkling wine or champagne, drain. Remove stems and slice strawberries. Toss all berries together in a bowl with sugar and Grand Marnier and let marinate for 1 hour. In two chilled wine goblets, place a scoop of frozen yogurt and top with berries.
Garnish: Fresh mint sprig.

The Menu

Seafood Fritters
A MIXTURE OF SHRIMP, CRAB MEAT AND SCALLOPS

Spaghettini with Tuna
SERVED IN A SPICY HOMEMADE TOMATO SAUCE

Veal Scaloppini
SEASONED WITH WHITE WINE AND FRESH SAGE

Bite Size Cream Puffs
FILLED WITH ITALIAN PASTRY CREAM

For a Little Romance:

For this dinner bring out your prettiest dishes, silverware, flower vases, candles, tablecloth and cloth napkins. Tie each napkin with a gold ribbon and a fresh rose or flower. Hide a handwritten love note inside the napkin. Paying attention to little details contribute to the pleasure one can get from a meal.

Let's Talk Wines For This Menu

Seafood Fritters
A MIXTURE OF SHRIMP, CRAB MEAT AND SCALLOPS

Wine Criteria:
The key ingredients are the egg batter and the fat in the oil for frying. Therefore, you need a light dry, unoaked, with high acidity white wine. The acidity in the wine should be able to cut through the fat.

Suggestions:
Muscadet de Sevre-et-Maine, Loire Valley (France) **$7**
Muscadet de Sevre-et-Maine "Sur Lies," Loire Valley (France) **$9**
(This is similar to the first choice, but has a little effervescence as a result of leaving the lies in the bottle, which makes an even better match.)
❤ Calera Viognier, Mt. Harlen (California) **$35**
(Select a younger vintage which possesses higher acidity)
Chablis A.C., Burgundy (France) **$20-$25**
(Select a village Chablis from a younger vintage rather than a Premier Cru or Grand Cru)

You can serve a light but dry sparkling wine from California or Spain. Serve the best wine you can afford, as the higher priced ones are drier with elegance that resembles the French style Champagnes.

Suggestions:
Aria Brut, Catalonia (Spain) **$8**
Domaine Carneros, Blanc de Blancs Brut, Carneros (California) **$16**
Iron Horse, Blanc de Blancs Brut, Sonoma County (California) **$21**
Scharffenberger Blanc de Blancs Brut, Anderson Valley (California) **$22**

❤ *Romantic Match/See Wine Glossary*

Spaghettini with Tuna
SERVED IN A SPICY TOMATO SAUCE

Wine Criteria:

Tuna is one of the most versatile fish to pair and enjoy with red wine, especially if it is grilled over aromatic wood medium rare. However, in the above dish grilled tuna is not used, instead the recipe calls for canned tuna and is served in a spicy tomato sauce which is an "acidic component." Therefore, in giving more attention to the spicy tomato sauce we suggest a white wine with aromatic, grassy and herbal flavors which will contrast the spiciness of the sauce beautifully. You could also serve an aromatic dry white with high acidity, however try to avoid the overly oaky whites.

Suggestions:

Cloudy Bay Sauvignon Blanc, Marborough, South Island (New Zealand) **$16**

Calera Viognier, Mt. Harlen (California) (2-3 year old) **$35**

Olivier Rully 1er Cru, Burgundy (France) select a recent vintage **$18**

Collio Sauvignon Blanc, Fruili-Venezia Guillia (Italy) **$15**

Sanford Sauvignon Blanc, Santa Barbara (California) **$9**

Veal Scaloppini
SEASONED WITH WHITE WINE AND FRESH SAGE

Wine Criteria:
This dish requires a full-bodied rich, oaky dry style white wine with good fruits such as, a high quality California Chardonnay. Choose a young Chardonnay from a good vintage, such as 1994, an excellent vintage rich in fruits, balanced with good acidity, especially from a good producer. A Premier Cru White Burgundy, or a Grand Cru Burgundy would also work.

Suggestions:
Beringer Reserve Chardonnay, Napa Valley, (California) **$25**
Calera Chardonnay, Mt. Harlen (California) **$16**
Edna Valley Chardonnay, San Luis Obispo (California) **$15**
Estacia Chardonnay, Monterey (California) **$10** *(bugdet choice and best value)*

If you are out to really impress a "wine snob" here is another suggestion:
Louis Latour (or any other producer) Le Montrachet, Burgundy, (France) **$200-$350**
Select one with a few years of age, i.e. 1988, 1986, 1985

Bite Size Cream Puffs
FILLED WITH ITALIAN PASTRY CREAM

Wine Criteria:
Select a botrytized-sweet white wine, such as a Sauternes from France. Although, a late harvest Riesling or Ice style wine from California will also work.

Suggestions:
Château Climents, Barsac (France) **$40**
Torcolato Maculan, Veneto (Italy) **$60**
Château Rieussec, Sauternes (France) **$60**

And if you must impress your "wine snob" all the way to the end try:
Zind-Humbrecht Tokay Pinot Gris "Clos St. Urbain Rangan"
Selection de Grains Nobles **$225 ¹/₂ bt**

Without worrying about impressing anyone but yourself!
Bonney Doon Orange Muscat, Santa Cruz (California) **$10 ¹/₂ bt** *budget choice*

One final thought:
Even though the wine selections listed above will match the dessert course perfectly, serving this rich dessert with wines so rich they are capable of thickening your blood just by thinking about them, leads me to think that you may want to choose the **Orange Muscat** *listed last under the Budget Choice. It will not only save you "lots a money," but it is a light and refreshing dessert wine, with a hint of orange to match the orange zest flavor in the dessert.*

The Recipes

Seafood Fritters

Little spoonfuls of minced shrimp, crab meat and scallops in a light batter make these appetizers a pleasure to your palate.

1/8 POUND FRESH SHRIMP, DE-VEINED, PEELED AND CHOPPED SMALL

1/8 POUND LUMP CRAB MEAT (FRESH OR CANNED)

1/8 POUND FRESH SEA SCALLOPS, CHOPPED SMALL

2 TABLESPOONS ONION, GRATED

1 TABLESPOON FRESH PARSLEY, CHOPPED FINE

1 CLOVE GARLIC, MINCED

1 EGG, BEATEN

1/4 CUP BREAD CRUMBS

2 TABLESPOONS FLOUR

1/2 TEASPOON SALT, PEPPER TO TASTE

1 TEASPOON MAYONNAISE

3 TABLESPOONS FRYING OIL (MAZOLA OR CANOLA)

1 LEMON, CUT IN WEDGES (FOR GARNISH)

Chop all ingredients and mix together with egg, bread crumbs, mayonnaise, salt and pepper. In a large frying pan, heat oil over medium high heat until hot. Using a large soup spoon, spoon out mixture into hot oil, flatten gently with the back of spoon. Brown on both sides, 3-4 minutes on each side. *Can be kept warm (uncovered) in a preheated oven at 200 degrees F.* Garnish: Lemon wedges.

Spaghettini with Tuna

A light piquant tomato sauce blends beautifully with tuna in this quick and easy pasta dish.

2 WHOLE CLOVES GARLIC

2 TABLESPOONS OLIVE OIL

1 -16 OZ. CAN PLUM TOMATOES, DRAINED AND CHOPPED

4 ANCHOVY FILETS

1-6 OUNCE CAN TUNA, IN WATER OR OIL

SALT AND PEPPER TO TASTE

1 DRIED RED HOT PEPPER

½ POUND SPAGHETTINI

3 QUARTS WATER

SALT TO TASTE

ITALIAN PARSLEY (FOR GARNISH)

In a large skillet, heat oil and sauté garlic until golden. Add anchovies and dried red pepper. Stir anchovies with a wooden spoon until dissolved. Add tuna and stir gently. Add tomatoes, salt and pepper. Simmer for 20 minutes.

Meanwhile in a large pot, bring 3 quarts water to boil and salt. Prepare pasta *"al dente."** Drain pasta, return it to the same pot. Pour sauce over and mix well. Serve in pasta bowls.

Garnish: Freshly chopped Italian parsley.

* *Literally translated, "al dente" means "to the tooth" or to the point where it is tender when bitten, but still offers slight resistance. Pasta cooked this way soaks up the savory sauces better than overcooked pasta.*

Veal Scaloppini

Unquestionably, the most popular of all Italian dishes are those made with veal scaloppini. Thin, tender slices of veal sautéed in garlic, white wine, fresh sage and a touch of cream. For the most tender scaloppini, buy a thicker piece of veal and pound it thin yourself. Here I will share with you the secrets for preparing the most tender scaloppini ever!

4 PIECES VEAL SCALOPPINI, POUNDED FLAT*

2 TABLESPOONS OLIVE OIL

2 TABLESPOONS FLOUR

2 WHOLE CLOVES GARLIC

1/4 CUP DRY WHITE WINE OR CHICKEN BROTH

3 SPRIGS FRESH SAGE

SALT AND PEPPER TO TASTE

2 TABLESPOONS FRESH CREAM (OPTIONAL)

The secret is the right cut of veal. The butcher must use the top round of veal in one solid piece and cut it against the grain to make the scaloppini. Unless they are cut this way, the scaloppini will toughen, shrink and curl when cooked. The scaloppini must then be pounded to a very thin consistency which also contributes to the delicacy of the dish.

Place each veal scaloppini in a plastic bag or between two layers of plastic wrap and pound with the flat side of a meat cleaver until very thin. *The proper pounding procedure is to bring the flat side of meat cleaver down on the center of the meat and slide from the center outward in one continuous motion. Do this until each scaloppini is thinned out evenly.* Salt and pepper lightly, then dust with flour.

Heat oil and garlic in a large frying pan, over medium high heat, until hot. Remove garlic cloves when golden, then raise the heat to high.

When oil is very hot, sauté veal very quickly, 30 seconds to 1 minute on each side. Do not over cook. Add white wine or chicken broth and 1 sprig fresh sage, cook for another minute. Add optional cream. Remove from pan and serve immediately.

Garnish: Fresh sage sprig.

Bite Size Cream Puffs

These little cream puffs filled with Italian pastry cream are truly a "party in your mouth." Bet you can't eat just one!

Cream Puff Shells

½ CUP WATER

½ STICK UNSALTED BUTTER

¼ TEASPOON SALT

½ CUP FLOUR

2 WHOLE EGGS (PREFERABLY AT ROOM TEMPERATURE)

Preheat oven to 375 degrees F. In a saucepan, bring water, butter and salt to boil over medium heat. Immediately remove the pan from the heat, then sift in the flour all at once. Stir until smooth and return to the heat. Cook, stirring for about 30 seconds. Remove from heat. Beat in eggs one at a time until mixture is smooth and has a shine to it.

On a greased baking sheet, drop a teaspoon of batter for each cream puff shell. This recipe yields 12-14 bite-size puffs. Place puffs in oven immediately, so batter is still warm when it enters oven. This will make the puffs light and airy. Bake at 375 degrees F for about 20 minutes, or until they have risen and are golden brown.

To test puffs for doneness, remove one from oven and cut open to be sure there is no unbaked paste on the inside. If there is, continue baking for another 5-7 minutes. When done, remove puffs to a rack and cool.

Place extra puffs in a plastic bag and refrigerate or freeze.

Italian Pastry Cream
3/4 CUP COLD MILK

1 EGG YOLK

3 TABLESPOONS SUGAR

2 TABLESPOONS FLOUR

1 CINNAMON STICK

1 TEASPOON ORANGE AND LEMON PEEL (ZEST)

OPTIONAL: USE ICE CREAM IN PLACE OF PASTRY CREAM

CHOCOLATE SAUCE AND/OR POWDERED SUGAR (FOR GARNISH)

In a saucepan, put cold milk, sugar, egg yolk and flour. Stir well with a wire whisk until flour is completely dissolved and there are no lumps.

Add cinnamon stick, orange and lemon peel. Continue cooking over medium high heat, stirring constantly until the mixture thickens. Remove from heat and discard cinnamon stick, orange and lemon peels. Cover the surface with plastic wrap and refrigerate until cold.

To prepare cream puffs, slice the top third off with a serrated knife. Spoon a generous amount of cooled Italian pastry cream into bottom portion of the puff. Replace top and refrigerate for up to 2 hours before serving.

Garnish: Chocolate sauce or sprinkle with powdered sugar.

Chocolate Sauce
3 OUNCES CHOCOLATE, CUT IN SMALL PIECES*

* *Use your favorite chocolate bar or chocolate chips.*

Place chocolate pieces in top of a double boiler, heat over medium high heat until chocolate melts.

The Menu

Pizza Capricciosa
FRESH MUSHROOMS, TOMATOES, MOZZARELLA, PROSCIUTTO AND ARUGULA

Ricotta Agnolotti
HOMEMADE CRESCENT SHAPED PASTA STUFFED WITH RICOTTA CHEESE
AND TOPPED WITH FRESH MARINARA SAUCE

Seared Salmon
TOPPED WITH FRESH TOMATOES, GARLIC, ANCHOVIES, CAPERS AND OLIVES

Tiramisù
LADYFINGERS SOAKED IN ESPRESSO, GRAND MARNIER AND
LAYERED WITH MASCARPONE & CREAM

For A Little Romance:

Let's make this dinner extra special by planning and cooking it together with your lover. Sit close and snuggle while you go over the recipes to make your shopping list. Go shopping together, hold hands to and from the store, and remember to kiss frequently while working together in the kitchen! Everything is easier when you are two.

Let's Talk Wines For This Menu

Pizza Capricciosa
FRESH MUSHROOMS, TOMATOES, MOZZARELLA, PROSCIUTTO AND ARUGULA

Wine Criteria:
Your key component here is the acidity in the tomatoes. Therefore, choose a young red wine from a warm climate that is fruity and low in tannin.

Suggestions:
Valpolicella Classico Superiore, Veneto (Italy) **$6-$10**
Atlas Peak Cosenso, Napa Valley (California) **$24**
Beaujolais Villages, Burgundy (France) **$6-$10**
Beaulieu Vineyard, Beteautor Cabernet Sauvignon, Napa Valley (California) **$10**
Rosemount Shiraz, Hunter Valley, New South Wales (Australia) **$10**
Concha Y Toro Cabernet/Merlot, Mapio (Chile) **$6**

Ricotta Agnolotti
CRESCENT SHAPED PASTA STUFFED WITH RICOTTA CHEESE
AND TOPPED WITH FRESH MARINARA SAUCE

Wine Criteria:
Select an unoaked, light-bodied, dry white wine, or an elegant style white that is slightly oaky with good acidity and a toasty finish.

Suggestions:
Soave Classico, Veneto (Italy) **$5-$8**
Orvieta Classico, Umbria (Italy) **$6-$8**
Gavi di Gavi "La Minaia", Piedmont (Italy) **$15-$20**
Pinot Blanc, Alsace (France) **$11-$15**
Muscadet de Sevre-et-Maine, Loire Valley (France) **$8**
Montagny "Premier Cru", Burgundy (France) **$21**
Pouilly Fuissé, Burgundy (France) **$15-$25**
Calera Voignier, Mt. Harlan (California) **$35**
Caymus Sauvignon Blanc, Napa Valley (California) **$14**
Clos du Bois Chardonnay, Sonoma County (California) **$10**
Château Musar, Ghazir (Lebanon) **$12**

Seared Salmon

TOPPED WITH FRESH TOMATOES, GARLIC, ANCHOVIES, CAPERS AND OLIVES

Wine Criteria:

The dominating flavors in this dish are the anchovies, capers, garlic and tomatoes that boost the acidity in the dish. Therefore, choose a dry grassy, aromatic white wine with high acidity and not too much oak.

Suggestions:

Domaine Thomas Sancerre, Loire Valley (France) **$15**

Côtes du Rhône Blanc, Rhône Valley (France) **$10**

❤ Cloudy Bay Sauvignon Blanc, Marlborough (New Zealand) **$15**

Avignonesi Il Vignola, Tuscany, (Italy) **$24**

Duckhorn Sauvignon Blanc, Napa Valley (California) **$13**

Château Musar Blanc, Ghazir (Lebanon) **$16**

Tiramisù

LADY FINGERS SOAKED IN ESPRESSO, GRAND MARNIER, AND LAYERED WITH MASCARPONE AND CREAM

Wine Criteria:

A late harvest, non-botrytized, sweet white wine, or a medium sweet to sweet white sparkling wine or Champagne.

Suggestions:

Vin Santo, Tuscany (Italy) **$35**

Moscato D'Asti, Piedmont (Italy) **$13**

Recioto di Soave, Veneto (Italy) **$20-$35**

NV Veuve Clicquot Demi-Sec, Champagne (France) **$33**

Hogue Cellars "Late Harvest" White Riesling, Yakima Valley (Washington State) **$12**

❤ *Romantic Match/See Wine Glossary*

Pizza Capricciosa

Capricciosa means "free and impulsive style," so why not let your imagination
and taste buds determine what you will put on this pizza.
The recipe below is a favorite (pictured on the front cover.)

Dough for Thinned Crust Pizza

1 CUP UNBLEACHED FLOUR

7 GRAMS OF DRY YEAST (1/2 PACKET)

1/2 CUP LUKEWARM WATER

1 TABLESPOON OLIVE OIL

1 TEASPOON SALT

In a medium size bowl, mix flour and salt together. In another bowl, mix 1/2 cup lukewarm water, yeast and oil. Let rest for 10 minutes. Add water and yeast to flour and mix together until it forms a ball. If it is too dry, add water; and if too wet, add flour. Cover the bowl with a towel, let rise for 1/2 hour to 1 hour. It can rest for 2-3 hours. Remove dough from bowl, knead on a flat floured surface until smooth. Add a little flour at a time if too sticky. Roll pizza dough out as thin as possible to fit a 12-14" round pizza screen. Place on the pizza screen and pinch crust edges with fingers. Brush dough with olive oil, including the edges.

Topping for Pizza

2 TABLESPOONS OLIVE OIL

1 CLOVE GARLIC, CHOPPED

½ TEASPOON DRIED OREGANO

3-4 LARGE FRESH PLUM TOMATOES, SLICED THIN

1-2 LARGE FRESH MOZZARELLA BALLS,* SLICED THIN

2 SLICES PROSCIUTTO, SLICED THIN AND CHOPPED

10 FRESH ARUGULA LEAVES, CHOPPED

SALT AND PEPPER TO TASTE

1 TABLESPOON PARMIGIANO REGGIANO OR PARMESAN CHEESE, FRESHLY GRATED

OPTIONAL: PINCH RED PEPPER FLAKES TO TASTE

* Fresh mozzarella looks like a hard boiled egg in water. It has a creamy delicate flavor that cannot be duplicated. It is available in specialty grocery stores or an Italian delicatessen.

Preheat oven to 450 degrees F. Marinate sliced tomatoes in olive oil, garlic, oregano, salt and pepper for 15-20 minutes. Break each tomato slice on one side and stretch it out placing it on top of pizza dough in a circular pattern until all tomato slices have been used. Then add fresh mozzarella ball slices, parmesan cheese, and optional red pepper flakes.

Bake for 10-15 minutes or until cheese is melted and crust is light golden brown on edges and bottom. Because oven temperatures vary, it is necessary to watch the pizza. When done, remove pizza from oven and place it on a cutting board. Let cool a few minutes before slicing.

Garnish: Sprinkle chopped arugula on top and place prosciutto in a mound in the center.

Be creative and experiment with different toppings!

Ricotta Agnolotti

These homemade crescent shaped dumplings stuffed with ricotta cheese filling are one of my most popular pasta dishes. They are so light, they literally melt in your mouth.

Homemade Pasta Dough for the Agnolotti

1 CUP FLOUR

1 EGG OR SUBSTITUTE WITH 2 EGG WHITES

1 TEASPOON SALT

1 TABLESPOON WATER, IF NEEDED

Using the metal blade of your food processor, combine egg and salt, and blend for 10 seconds; then add flour quickly through the feed tube. Continue mixing until mixture forms a ball (about 5-10 seconds until machine slows down or stops).

Note: If the dough is too dry, add water; if too soft, add flour and knead into dough.

Wrap dough in plastic wrap, let rest for ¹/₂ hour to 3 hours. During this time you can prepare Tomato Sauce and Ricotta Filling.

Tomato Sauce

2 CUPS FRESH OR CANNED ITALIAN PLUM TOMATOES, DRAINED AND CRUSHED*

1 CLOVE GARLIC, CRUSHED

6 LEAVES FRESH BASIL, CHOPPED

2 TABLESPOONS OLIVE OIL

¹/₂ TEASPOON SALT

PEPPER TO TASTE

* Do not buy crushed canned tomatoes. Always buy whole tomatoes. Drain tomatoes and crush them by hand (or in a food processor for 3-5 seconds) because the crushed canned tomatoes will make the sauce too thick.

In a skillet, heat the oil and garlic over medium heat until golden, then add the tomatoes, salt and pepper and basil. Simmer for 20 minutes.

Prepare Filling

½ POUND RICOTTA CHEESE

¼ CUP PARMIGIANO-REGGIANO OR PARMESAN CHEESE

PINCH FRESHLY GRATED NUTMEG

¼ CUP CHOPPED ITALIAN PARSLEY

¼ CUP PLAIN BREAD CRUMBS

1 EGG

¼ TEASPOON SALT

Mix the ricotta thoroughly with all the ingredients. Set aside until ready to fill agnolotti.

Preparing and Assembling the Agnolotti
Agnolottis are half moon shape raviolis

3 QTS. WATER

1 TEASPOON SALT

FRESH BASIL LEAVES (FOR GARNISH)

When you unwrap dough, it will seem more moist than it did originally. Do not add any more flour. Dust your hands with flour and knead dough for 1 minute.

Roll out dough using a hand-cranked pasta machine. Set rollers of pasta maker at their maximum opening. Run dough through 3 or 4 times, folding and turning it each time you feed it through. Then close the opening one notch, and run dough through once. Continue closing the opening one notch at a time and feed dough (pasta ribbon) through the rollers once each time until the lowest notch is reached and dough is very thin. **See diagram on next page.** *Note: If the dough gets too sticky, dust with a little flour.*

Cut dough into circles about 4" in diameter using a cookie cutter or mouth of a large glass. Place a little of filling mixture on one half of each circle. Fold the other half over filling. Pinch edges with the tines of a fork. If edges get dry, dampen them with water or egg wash.

Bring a large pot of water to boil and add salt. Cook the agnolotti in gently boiling salted water for about 3-5 minutes or until they float. Carefully remove them with a slotted spoon and drain. Arrange 3 or 5 agnolotti on individual plates, serve with fresh tomato sauce.

Garnish: Fresh basil leaves.

Diagram #4

Diagram #3

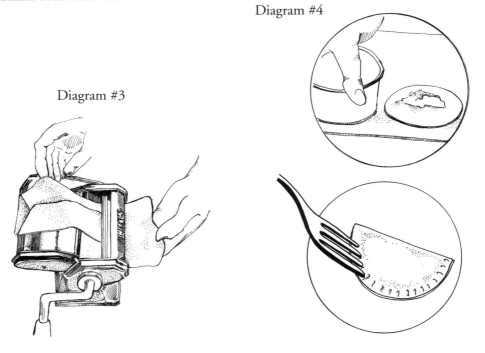

Seared Salmon with Zesty Tomato Sauce

Salmon is a wonderful fish to sear. There is no simpler or more delicious way to prepare it. You've got to try this recipe.

2- 8 OUNCE PIECES FRESH SALMON FILET WITH SKIN ON ONE SIDE

3 TABLESPOONS OLIVE OIL

1 CLOVE GARLIC

Heat olive oil and garlic over medium heat until garlic turns golden. Remove and discard. Raise heat to high. When oil is hot, place salmon filets in hot oil, skin side down, and sear. Stand back so hot oil doesn't splatter on you. Cover, turn heat down to medium, and cook for approximately 10 minutes. Do not turn over.

Zesty Tomato Sauce

2 MEDIUM SIZE FRESH PLUM TOMATOES, DICED

1 SMALL CLOVE GARLIC, CHOPPED

2 ANCHOVY FILETS

1 OUNCE BLACK OLIVES,* PITTED AND SLICED

1 TABLESPOON CAPERS

SALT AND PEPPER TO TASTE

1 TABLESPOON OLIVE OIL

2 SPRIGS ITALIAN PARSLEY FOR GARNISH

* *Use the Greek Kalamata olives or the imported Niçoise olives, these type olives are much more flavorful.*

In a medium size saucepan, heat olive oil and garlic over medium heat until garlic is golden. Add anchovies and stir with a wooden spoon until dissolved. Add tomatoes, olives and capers. Salt and pepper to taste. Simmer for a few minutes. Spoon over salmon.

Garnish: Fresh Italian parsley sprigs.

Tiramisù

The ever popular Italian dessert is easier than you think,
and sure to keep your lover faithful!

14-16 LADYFINGER BISCUITS

4 OUNCES MASCARPONE* OR RICOTTA CHEESE

1 WHOLE EGG, SEPARATED

1 OUNCE SUGAR

4 OUNCES ESPRESSO OR VERY STRONG COFFEE, COOLED

1 CUP FRESHLY WHIPPED CREAM

2 TABLESPOONS COCOA POWDER

2 TABLESPOONS GRAND MARNIER

1 OUNCE MARSALA WINE

1 TABLESPOON CHOCOLATE SHAVINGS (FOR GARNISH)

* Mascarpone is the rich Italian cream cheese usually found in Italian specialty stores.

Prepare espresso, add 1 tablespoon sugar and let cool. Next add Grand Marnier to the coffee. Using a double boiler, bring water to boil in the bottom part. Place egg yolk, sugar and Marsala wine in top part of double boiler. Stir continuously, for 10 minutes or until mixture thickens. Remove from heat and cool. Meanwhile, beat egg white until stiff, set aside. Whip cream and set aside.

Fold mascarpone into egg mixture, then fold in beaten egg white and set aside. Brush ladyfingers generously, on one side only, with espresso and Grand Marnier. Do not soak. Line bottom of a small baking dish (approximately 10" X10") with half the ladyfingers, and spread with half the mascarpone mixture. Add a layer of freshly whipped cream and sprinkle with cocoa powder. Top with remaining ladyfingers. Spread remaining mascarpone mixture over ladyfingers. Finish with a layer of whipped cream. Refrigerate for at least 6 hours before serving.

Garnish: Chocolate shavings and a sprinkle of cocoa powder.

The Menu

Caesar Salad
HEARTS OF ROMAINE TOSSED WITH TRADITIONAL CAESAR DRESSING

Pasta with Zucchini and Shitake Mushrooms
SAUTÉED ZUCCHINI AND SHITAKE MUSHROOMS TOSSED IN A FRESH TOMATO SAUCE

Grilled Lamb Chops
MARINATED IN ROSEMARY AND GARLIC

Stuffed Apple Wrapped in Phyllo
SUGAR, CINNAMON AND ALMOND FILLING

For a Little Romance:

You've got to plan for romance, so give yourself plenty of time. Make a list, assemble all the ingredients for the menu, and do as much as you can ahead of time. Have the house sparkling clean, the table beautifully set, the candles lit, and the music playing. Remember planning doesn't destroy spontaneity, it creates opportunities.

Let's Talk Wines For This Menu

Caesar Salad

HEARTS OF ROMAINE TOSSED WITH TRADITIONAL CAESAR DRESSING

Wine Critera:
You can serve a light-bodied, dry sparkling wine from California, or Washington State.

Suggestions:
Domaine Ste. Michelle Blanc de Blancs Brut, Columbia Valley (Washington State) **$9**
Vintage Iron Horse Blanc de Blancs Brut, Sonoma Valley (California) **$25**
Domaine Carneros Blanc de Blancs Brut, Carneros (California) **$22**
Or try a Cremant style sparkling wine from California or from the Cremant de Bourgogne, appellation in Burgundy, France. These sparkling wines are light, dry with impressive fruits, and tend to get richer and more mellow with 3 to 5 years of age.

Suggestions:
Sancerre, Loire Valley (France) **$16**
Domaine Thibault Pouilly-Fumé, Loire Valley (France) **$20**
Avignonesi Il Vignola, Tuscany (Italy) **$26**
Boschendal Sauvignon Blanc, Stellenbosch (South Africa) **$13**
Duckhorn Sauvignon Blanc, Napa Valley (California) **$12**
Gamla Sauvignon Blanc, Golan Heights (Israel) **$14**

*If you would like to start the evening with an impressive statement, and you have set a big budget for this dinner, serve a **Salon Blanc de Blancs Brut, Champagne (France)** - select from older vintages, such as 69, 71, 73, 76, 79 or 82) price range $200 - $400. (It is a light, dry, and elegant Champagne with fine fruit richness that becomes increasingly apparent with age. It also develops a creamy silky finish.)*

Pasta with Zucchini and Shitake Mushrooms
SAUTÉED ZUCCHINI AND SHITAKE MUSHROOMS TOSSED IN A FRESH TOMATO SAUCE

Wine Criteria:
You may choose a style of white wine produced from Sauvignon Blanc grapes described in the selections of the first course. Or if the mushrooms were featured strongly in the recipe, select a cool climate, medium-bodied Red, such as California, Oregon, or even a Red Burgundy from the Côtes de Beaume. These wines possess good acidity to counter the acidity in the tomato sauce, and the velvety texture that match the earthiness of the mushrooms, and the zucchini.

Suggestions:
Sanford Pinot Noir, Central Coast (California) **$20**
Saintsbury Pinot Noir, Carneros (California) **$16**
Alsace Pinot Noir, Alsace, (France) Rare and hard to find **$30-$40**
Haut Côtes de Beaume, Burgundy (France) **$24**
Domaine Joblot Givry, Burgundy (France) **$20**
Ponzi Pinot Noir, Wilamette Valley (Oregon) **$17**
Knudsen-Erath Pinot Noir, Willamette Valley (Oregon) **$14**

Grilled Lamb Chops
MARINATED IN ROSEMARY AND GARLIC

Wine Criteria:
It's a practice among wine experts and gourmands that if you want to highlight a good old bottle of Bordeaux or even Burgundy, serve it with grilled lamb chops. It is the traditional vehicle for a good red Bordeaux. Having said that, I would serve a red wine with elegance and complexity.

Suggestions:
Joseph Phelps Insignia, Napa Valley (California) **$55**
Robert Mondavi Reserve Cabernet Sauvignon, Napa Valley (California) **$55 -$100**
(Select the older Vintages i.e. '74, '78, '80, '82, '86)
Opus One, Napa Valley (California) **$75**
Château Lafite Rothschild Pauillac, Bordeaux (France) **$100 -$300**
Wolf Blass "Yellow Label" Cabernet Sauvignon, S. Australia (Australia) **$10** *budget choice*
Château La Rose-Trianaudon, Bordeaux (France) **$12** *budget choice*

Stuffed Apple Wrapped in Phyllo
SUGAR, CINNAMON AND ALMOND FILLING

Wine Criteria:
Choose a botrytized-sweet white wine such as a Sauternes from Bordeaux, France or a Vindage Tardive style Riesling or Gewurztraminer. A budget choice would be a late harvest style Riesling from California.

Suggestions:
Fetzer "Late Harvest" Riesling, Mendocino County (California) **$9**
Château Climents, Bordeaux (France) **$50**
Maculan Torcolato, Veneto (Italy) **$60**
Tokaji Aszu "5 Puttonyos," Tokaj-Hegyalja (Hungary) **$25**

The Recipes

Caesar Salad

Worthy of its name, this salad is a classic that never loses its appeal.
The secret is the dressing and homemade croutons.

2 CUPS ROMAINE LETTUCE HEARTS

Wash the lettuce, dry well and tear into bite-size pieces. Set aside.

Caesar Dressing

1 SMALL CLOVE GARLIC, CRUSHED

3 FILETS ANCHOVIES, CRUSHED

¼ CUP OLIVE OIL

1 MEDIUM EGG YOLK, CODDLED (OPTIONAL)

3-4 DASHES TOBASCO

BLACK PEPPER FRESHLY GROUND TO TASTE

SALT TO TASTE

2-3 DASHES WORCESTERSHIRE SAUCE

1 TABLESPOON FRESH LEMON JUICE

1 TABLESPOON DIJON MUSTARD

3 TABLESPOONS PARMIGIANO-REGGIANO OR PARMESAN CHEESE,
FRESHLY GRATE 2 TABLESPOONS AND

SHAVE 1 TABLESPOON WITH A VEGETABLE PEELER (FOR GARNISH)

If using egg yolk, coddle it in a small bowl of warm water for 10 minutes. Combine crushed garlic and anchovies and make a paste, add Worcestershire sauce, mustard, tobasco, lemon juice, grated parmesan cheese, black pepper and egg yolk. Whisk in oil slowly and continue whisking until thoroughly blended.

Homemade Croutons

1 CUP DAY OLD ITALIAN OR FRENCH BREAD, CUT IN 1" CUBES

3 TABLESPOONS OLIVE OIL

1 WHOLE CLOVE GARLIC

$\frac{1}{2}$ TEASPOON DRIED OREGANO

$\frac{1}{2}$ TEASPOON DRIED BASIL

1 TEASPOON PARMESAN CHEESE

In a skillet, heat oil and garlic over medium heat until garlic is golden. Toss bread cubes with herbs and cheese and add to heated oil and garlic. Stir until golden brown. Remove from pan and place on a paper towel to absorb any excess oil.

Toss lettuce, croutons and dressing until all leaves are coated. Serve immediately on cold salad plates. Make cheese shavings with a vegetable peeler for garnish.

Garnish: Freshly grated Parmesan cheese shavings.

Pasta with Zucchini, Mushrooms & Fresh Tomato Sauce

This simple and elegant pasta dish is light, colorful and very tasty.
Remember it is essential to use the freshest ingredients.

1 MEDIUM ZUCCHINI, JULIENNED*

8 OUNCES FRESH SHITAKE MUSHROOMS, SLICED THIN

1 MEDIUM ONION, CHOPPED

1-16 OUNCE CAN OF TOMATOES WITH JUICE, CHOPPED

2 WHOLE CLOVES GARLIC

SALT AND PEPPER TO TASTE

½ POUND ANGEL HAIR PASTA, OR SPAGHETTINI PASTA, COOKED AL DENTE

2 TABLESPOONS FRESHLY PARMIGIANO-REGGIANO OR PARMESAN CHEESE

3 TABLESPOONS OLIVE OIL

OPTIONAL: PINCH RED PEPPER FLAKES

Julienne means to cut into short thin strips ⅛" across

In a skillet, heat 2 tablespoons olive oil and garlic over medium heat, add onions and sauté until golden. Raise heat to medium high and add mushrooms. Sauté quickly until they are golden brown, then add zucchini and cook another 5 minutes until zucchini has turned a nice green color. Add salt. *(Reserve 4 tablespoons of the zucchini, onions and mushrooms for garnish),* then add tomatoes and juice. Simmer for 20 minutes. Remove whole garlic cloves before serving.

Meanwhile, cook angel hair pasta *"al dente."* Drain and return to cooking pan. Toss thoroughly with vegetable sauce and 1 tablespoon parmesan cheese. Serve in pasta bowls.

Garnish: Reserved vegetables, and sprinkle with remaining Parmigiano-Reggiano/ parmesan cheese.

Grilled Lamp Chops with Rosemary & Garlic

Easy and so delicious, these lamb chops have been called by many…. the world's best!

4 LAMB CHOPS (USE LOIN) CUT, MEDIUM THICK

2 TABLESPOONS OLIVE OIL

1 CLOVE GARLIC, CRUSHED

1 SPRIG FRESH ROSEMARY, CHOPPED FINE

1 TABLESPOON BALSAMIC VINEGAR

$1/2$ TEASPOON SALT

PEPPER TO TASTE

2 SPRIGS FRESH ROSEMARY, LEAVE WHOLE (FOR GARNISH)

Mix oil, chopped garlic, chopped fresh rosemary, salt, pepper, and balsamic vinegar in a small bowl . Brush mixture on both sides of lamb chops. Marinate for 1 hour. Grill lamb chops until brown (about 7 minutes a side) or until medium rare. Do not overcook.

Garnish: Whole sprigs of fresh rosemary.

Stuffed Apple Wrapped in Phyllo Dough

This dessert is an opulent treatment for apples. Here they are baked whole with a toasted almond stuffing in layers of light phyllo crust. An added bonus is the whole house smells as delicious as these apples taste!

2 MEDIUM ROME APPLES, PEELED AND CORED

2 TABLESPOONS LEMON JUICE

1/4 CUP BROWN SUGAR

1/2 TEASPOON CINNAMON

1/4 STICK BUTTER, MELTED OR

1/4 CUP CANOLA OIL

6 LARGE SHEETS PHYLLO DOUGH, LARGE SHEETS, CUT TO 8" X 10" PIECES

1/4 CUP TOASTED ALMONDS, CHOPPED

2 SCOOPS FROZEN VANILLA YOGURT

1 TABLESPOON POWERED SUGAR (FOR GARNISH)

OPTIONAL: MELTED CHOCOLATE (FOR GARNISH)

Follow instructions on phyllo dough package; if frozen, thaw ahead of time. Peel and core apples; set aside in a bowl of cold water and lemon juice.

Preheat oven to 350 degrees F. In a bowl, mix brown sugar, cinnamon, and toasted almonds. Lay phyllo sheets out on flat surface. Brush butter or oil over each sheet of phyllo dough and sprinkle with some sugar mixture. Make 3 layers. Place apple in center of phyllo dough layers and fill core with remaining sugar mixture. Place one corner of phyllo dough over top of apple and brush with butter. Repeat with all the corners. Turn apple over in a small baking bowl and brush with butter. Bake uncovered for 30-40 minutes until golden brown and apple is done. Serve warm.

Garnish: Small scoop of "melted" frozen vanilla yogurt on each plate, placing baked apple on top. If using chocolate, melt chocolate and drizzle over. Dust with powered sugar.

The Menu

Anchovy & Black Olive Crostini
FRESH MOZZARELLA, ANCHOVIES, CAPERS AND BLACK OLIVES

Seafood Ravioli with Roasted Red Pepper Sauce
RAVIOLI STUFFED WITH SALMON, SHRIMP AND SCALLOPS,
TOPPED WITH ROASTED RED PEPPER CREAM SAUCE

Veal Milanese
BREADED VEAL CUTLETS TOPPED WITH FRESH TOMATOES, GARLIC & ARUGULA

Macedonia
FRESH MIXED FRUIT MARINATED IN LEMON JUICE AND GRAND MARNIER

For A Little Romance:

Plan a "Dress for Dinner Night." Write an invitation to your lover to "Dine-In," giving the date, the time, the place, and request formal attire only. Wear something very sexy. Remember men are very stimulated by what they see. Be sure all the details are purrr…fect!

Let's Talk Wines For This Menu

Anchovy and Black Olive Crostini
FRESH MOZZARELLA, ANCHOVIES CAPERS AND BLACK OLIVES

Wine Criteria:
This dish has two important components that you need to consider, the salty anchovies, and the acidic capers. Therefore you need a dry, aromatic white wine with good acidity. Or even try a grassy, aromatic, dry white, such as a California Sauvignon Blanc or a Pouilly Fumé from the Loire Valley in France. Whatever your choice may be from the above mentioned criteria, choose one that has good acidity with a dry finish and subtle fruits.

Suggestions:
Santa Margharita Pinot Grigio, Veneto (Italy) **$20**
Avignonesi Il Vignola, Tuscany (Italy) **$22**
Boschendal Sauvignon Blanc, Stellenbosch (South Africa) **$14**
Cloudy Bay Sauvignon Blanc, Marlborough, South Island (New Zealand) **$16**
Duckhorn Sauvignon Blanc, Napa Valley (California) **$15**
Frogs Leap Sauvignon Blanc, Napa Valley (California) **$8**

Or surprise your guest with this very interesting match:
Croft (or similar light style producer) Manzenilla Sherry (Spain) **$12**
It is a style of Sherry that is very dry, light and crisp, with a hint of salty tang which will match the salty anchovies.

Seafood Ravioli with Roasted Red Pepper Sauce
RAVIOLI STUFFED WITH SALMON, SHRIMP AND SCALLOPS, TOPPED WITH ROASTED RED PEPPER SAUCE

Wine Criteria:

The sauce in the dish is your key element, not the seafood. It has a velvety texture, and a peppery flavor. Therefore, your best match....believe it or not, is a dry, soft, spicy red wine, with a moderate oaky finish. The simpler and less complex the wine, the better the match, as the sauce will enhance the wine. However, if you feel that your guest is going to be offended because you are breaking an old stale rule, white wine with seafood, you may serve an unoaked, fruity, dry white wine after you have proved them wrong!

Suggestions: (Red)

❤ Acinum Valpolicella Classico, Veneto (Italy) **$9**

Domaine Capion Syrah, Provence (France) **$8**

Andru Brunnel Côtes du Rhône, Rhône Valley (France) **$10**

Suggestions: (White)

Chalone Chenin Blanc, Monterey (California) **$16**

Domaine Thomas Sancerre, Loire Valley (France) **$16**

Jermann Vintage Tunina, Friuli-Venezia Giulia (Italy) **$45**

Kenwood Sauvingnon Blanc, Sonoma (California) **$10**

❤ *Romantic Match/See Wine Glossary*

Veal Milanese

BREADED VEAL CUTLETS TOPPED WITH FRESH TOMATOES, GARLIC AND ARUGULA

Wine Criteria:
A delicately flavored dish that requires either a cool climate, medium-bodied red with a fairly good acidity, fruit and velvety finish.

Suggestions: (Red)
Valpolicella Classico Superior, Veneto (Italy) **$9-$12**
Barnard-Griffin Cabernet/Merlot, Columbia Valley (Washington State) **$16**
Sanford Pinot Noir, Central Coast (California) **$20**
Cain Five Meritage, Napa Valley (California) **$35**
Corton Clos du Rio, Burgundy (France) **$35**
Aldo Conterno Delcetto d'Alba, Piedmont, (Italy) 1991,'92,'93 **$17**

Or try a medium-bodied, dry, unoaked white with crisp acidity, and good fruits.
Suggestions: (White)
Santa Margharita Pinot Grigio, Veneto (Italy) **$20**
Zemmer Pinot Grigio, Friuli-Venezia Guilia (Italy) **$10**
Tokay Pinot Gris, Alsace (France) **$15-$30**
Note: A big style Chardonnay, or a Grand Cru Burgundy will overpower the dish.

Macedonia

IF USING TROPICAL FRUITS SUCH AS PINAPPLES, MANGOS, PAPAYA AND MELONS

Wine Criteria:

A simple dessert that requires a light style dessert wine with good acidity. Although, a little sweet style bubbly could enhance your dessert, as well as your romantic opportunity!

Suggestions:

Bonny Doon Orange Muscat, Santa Cruz (California) **$14 ¹/₂ bt**
Quady Elysium Black Muscat, Central Valley (California) **$20 ¹/₂ bt**
Muscat de Beaumes-de-Venise, Rhône Valley (France) **$13 ¹/₂ bt**
Moscato d'Asti, Piedmont (Italy) **$12-$15 ¹/₂ bt**

Macedonia

IF USING PEACHES, APRICOTS, AND NECTARINES

Wine Criteria:

Select a rich sweet white wine with good acidity, such as a Sauternes (a delicious combination) or a dry Rosé Champagne or Sparkling Wine since the dryness of the Champagne will set off the richness of the fruits.

Suggestions:

Torcolato Maculan, Veneto (Italy) **$65**
Tokaji Aszu "5 Puttonyos", Tokaj-Hegyalja (Hungary) **$45**
Chateau Climents, Barsac (France) **$55**
Chateau d'Yquem, Sauternes (France) **$100** and up ¹/₂ bottle depending on the vintage

Champagne & Sparkling Wine Suggestions:

(Non Vintage) NV Mumms Cuvée Napa Brut Rosé, Napa Valley (California) **$20**
(Non Vintage) NV Piper Sonoma Brut Rosé, Sonoma (California) **$35**
(Vintage) Bollinger Grand Anne Rosé, Champagne (France) **$120**
(Vintage) Iron Horse Brut Rosé, Sonoma (California) **$25**

The Recipes

Anchovy and Black Olive Crostini

Italian bread grilled with fresh mozzarella and a savory spread of anchovies, black olives, tiny green capers and fresh garlic

Topping:

4 ANCHOVY FILETS, LARGE BONES REMOVED

1 TABLESPOON CAPERS

1 TABLESPOON OLIVE OIL

1 SMALL CLOVE FRESH GARLIC, MINCED FINE

1/4 CUP BLACK OLIVES (GREEK) PITTED, CHOPPED

2 TABLESPOONS DRY WHITE WINE

Crostini:

4 SLICES FRESH MOZZARELLA CHEESE BALL,* SLICED THIN

1/4 LOAF GOOD CRUSTY COUNTRY ITALIAN OR FRENCH BREAD (A BAGUETTE WORKS FINE)

CUT INTO 4 1/2" THICK SLICES

2 SPRIGS FRESH ITALIAN PARSLEY (FOR GARNISH)

Fresh mozzarella looks like a hard boiled egg in water. It has a creamy delicate flavor that cannot be duplicated. It is available in specialty grocery stores or an Italian delicatessen.

Preheat broiler. Slice bread into 1/2" thick slices, set aside. Peel and mince fresh garlic, chop black olives. In a small saucepan, over medium high heat, add oil and garlic. Stir until garlic is golden. Then add anchovy filets, mash them with a wooden spoon, add wine, capers and olives. Simmer for 5 minutes.

Place a thin slice of fresh mozzarella cheese on top of each slice of bread. Place under broiler until cheese melts. Spoon small amount of sauce over melted cheese on each piece of bread. Serve immediately.

Garnish: Sprig of fresh Italian Parsley.

Seafood Ravioli with Roasted Red Pepper Sauce

An irresistible stuffed seafood pasta topped with a velvety roasted red pepper sauce

Homemade Pasta Dough for Ravioli

1 CUP FLOUR

1 WHOLE EGG AND 1 EGG WHITE

1 TEASPOON SALT

1 TABLESPOON WATER, IF NEEDED

In a food processor, insert the metal blade, mix eggs, add salt and blend for 10 seconds, then add flour quickly through the feed tube, continue blending until the mixture forms a ball about (5-10 seconds until machine slows down or stops). *If dough is too dry, add water; if too soft, add flour and knead into dough.*

Wrap dough in plastic wrap, set in a cool place for 45 minutes to 1 hour. During this time you can prepare the filling and roasted red pepper sauce.

Seafood Filling

2 OUNCES FRESH SALMON, SKIN REMOVED

8 LARGE JUMBO SHRIMP, PEELED AND DE-VEINED

2 TABLESPOONS OLIVE OIL

1 CLOVE GARLIC, CHOPPED

1 TABLESPOON FRESH PARSLEY CHOPPED FINE

$1/2$ TEASPOON SALT, PEPPER TO TASTE

1 WHOLE EGG OR 2 EGG WHITES

In a skillet, heat oil and garlic over medium heat. Add shallots and sauté until golden. Add salmon and shrimp, sauté for 3-4 minutes. Salt and pepper. Remove from heat, let cool, then chop. Add parsley and egg to chopped seafood, mix thoroughly, then set aside.

Red Pepper Sauce

2 LARGE SWEET RED PEPPERS, ROASTED AND PURÉED

1 SMALL SHALLOT, MINCED

1 CLOVE GARLIC, MINCED

1 TABLESPOON OLIVE OIL

SALT AND PEPPER TO TASTE

4 TABLESPOONS CREAM

Grill or broil red peppers on a foil-lined baking sheet until skins are black on all sides.

Place peppers in a plastic bag until cool enough to handle. Pull off charred skin and remove core and seeds. Purée peppers in a food processor or blender, add salt and pepper. Set aside.

In a small saucepan or skillet, heat oil, add garlic and shallots, and sauté until golden brown. Add pureed peppers, sauté for a few more minutes, then add cream. Heat until hot. Remove from heat. The sauce is ready.

Assembling and Serving the Ravioli

3 QUARTS WATER

1 TEASPOON SALT

FRESH BASIL OR ITALIAN PARSLEY (FOR GARNISH)

When you unwrap the pasta dough, it will seem more moist than it did originally. Do not add any more flour. Dust your hands with flour and knead dough for 1 minute. Divide dough into 2 parts. Flatten each piece with palm of your hand.

Roll out dough using a hand-cranked pasta machine. Set rollers of pasta maker at the maximum opening. Run dough through 3 or 4 times, folding and turning it each time you feed it through. Then close the opening one notch, and run dough through once. Continue closing the opening one notch at a time. Feed pasta ribbon through the rollers once each time until the lowest notch is reached. **See diagram #3 on page 66.** If dough becomes too sticky, dust with flour.

Cut rolled out pasta dough into large rectangles. *This shape, when filled, will make ravioli squares.* Put a spoonful of seafood filling to right or left of center. Brush edges of dough with water or egg wash, and fold over, pinch edges closed with tines of a fork. Place filled ravioli on a cotton cloth until ready to cook. **See diagram below.**

Bring a large pot of water to boil. Add 1 tablespoon of salt. Carefully drop the ravioli into gently boiling water. Cook ravioli in boiling water for about 4 minutes or until they float whichever comes first. Remove from boiling water with a slotted spoon. Drain well.

Serve a large spoonful of roasted red pepper sauce on 2 individual plates. Arrange 3 or 5 ravioli on top of sauce. Then finish with another spoonful of sauce.

Garnish: Fresh Italian parsley or basil.

Diagram #5

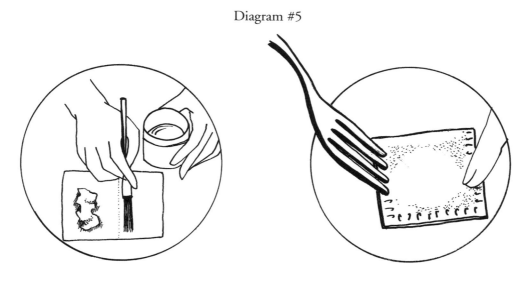

Veal Milanese

Tender and juicy breaded veal cutlets, topped with fresh tomatoes and arugula

TWO 1" THICK VEAL RIB CHOPS WITH BONE IN, BUTTERFLY

¼ CUP PLAIN BREAD CRUMBS

1 EGG, BEATEN

2 TABLESPOONS MILK

1 LARGE PLUM TOMATO, CHOPPED FINE

4 TABLESPOONS OLIVE OIL

2 SMALL CLOVES GARLIC, 1 CHOPPED FINE, 1 WHOLE

SALT AND PEPPER TO TASTE

8 ARUGULA LEAVES, CHOPPED (FOR GARNISH)

Mix together chopped tomato, 1 tablespoon oil, 1 small clove minced garlic, salt and pepper. Let marinate for 1/2 hour to 1 hour.

To butterfly the veal chop, slice the 1" thick veal chop in half, horizontally, until you reach the bone. Leave the bone intact. On a cutting board pull the two sides out flat to resemble a butterfly. Place veal between two sheets of plastic wrap and pound thin with flat side of a meat cleaver. Salt and pepper both sides of veal.

Diagram #6

Beat the egg with milk in a bowl large enough to dip veal cutlets.

Dip veal in egg mixture and then bread crumbs. Push bread crumbs into veal with the palm of your hand.

In a large skillet, heat 3 tablespoons olive oil and 1 whole garlic over medium high heat until garlic is golden. Remove and discard. Turn heat to high. When hot, sauté veal quickly on both sides until golden brown, 3-4 minutes. Remove from pan and place on paper towel to absorb excess oil. Place in baking dish and keep warm in oven at **250 degrees F**. until ready to serve for up to $1/2$ hour.

Garnish: Fresh chopped arugula and tomato marinade.

Macedonia

A simple fruit salad is elevated to an elegant dessert status with the addition of Grand Marnier and a few teaspoons of sugar and lemon.

4 FRESH STRAWBERRIES, RINSE AND DRAIN, CUT IN SMALL PIECES

3 TABLESPOONS FRESH RASPBERRIES, RINSED AND DRAINED

3 TABLESPOONS FRESH BLUEBERRIES, RINSED AND DRAINED

1 SMALL APPLE, DICED SMALL

1 BANANA, CUT IN SMALL PIECES

1 KIWI FRUIT, DICED SMALL

10 GRAPES

$\frac{1}{2}$ FRESH LEMON, JUICE OF

$\frac{1}{4}$ CUP GRAND MARNIER

4 TEASPOONS SUGAR

$\frac{1}{3}$ CUP WHITE WINE OR CHAMPAGNE

Rinse berries in a small amount of white wine or champagne, then place all the fruit together in a bowl, add sugar, Grand Marnier, lemon juice, and gently mix everything together. Marinate for one hour or more.

Garnish: Sprig of fresh mint.

Note: If these fresh berries are not all available, use any fresh fruit in season, include pineapples, mangos, papaya and melons.

Fresh Mozzarella Balls with Pesto
BITE-SIZE MOZZARELLA BALLS MARINATED IN BASIL PESTO SAUCE

Vegetable Lasagna
HOMEMADE LASAGNA NOODLES WITH FRESH VEGETABLES, RICOTTA CHEESE,
PARMESAN CHEESE AND FRESH TOMATO SAUCE

Sautéed Chicken Breasts
SIMMERED IN BALSAMIC VINEGAR AND FRESH ROSEMARY

Zuccotto alla Ricotta
SEMI-FROZEN LADYFINGER DOME FILLED WITH CREAM AND NUTS

For A Little Romance:

Serve this dinner in an unusual place. Set up a table next to the fireplace, or in a room you normally would not eat in. Make it elegant and romantic with table linens, flowers and candles. Cover the ceiling with white helium filled balloons with beautiful ribbons hanging from them. Tie white cut out hearts or snowflakes to the bottom of the ribbons.

Let's Talk Wines For This Menu

Fresh Mozzarella Balls with Pesto
BITE-SIZE MOZZARELLA BALLS MARINATED IN BASIL PESTO SAUCE

Wine Criteria:
Unoaked, light, dry white wine that is fruity and herbal with a crisp acidity.

Suggestions:
Calera Viognier, Mt. Harlan (California) **$35**
Chalone Chenin Blanc, Monterey (California) **$15**
Kenwood Sauvignon Blanc, Sonoma (California) **$10**
Château Musar Blanc, Ghazir (Lebanon) **$16**
Côtes du Rhône Blanc, Rhône Valley (France) **$10**
Pinot Blanc, Alsace (France) **$10-$12**
Riesling Italico Gravner, Friuli-Venezia Guilia (Italy) **$10**
Gruner Veltliner Ried Zwirch, Donauland (Austria) **$15**

Vegetable Lasagna
HOMEMADE NOODLES WITH FRESH VEGETABLES, RICOTTA CHEESE,
PARMESAN CHEESE AND HOMEMADE TOMATO SAUCE

Wine Criteria and Suggestions:
Select a wine from the style described in the first course.

Sautéed Chicken Breasts
SIMMERED IN BALSAMIC VINEGAR WITH FRESH ROSEMARY AND TOMATOES

Wine Criteria:
In this dish, you need to pay attention to two elements; the strong flavor of the rosemary, and the acidity of the tomatoes and the balsamic vinegar. Therefore you have two options – either match by components or by flavors.

1) *If you're going to match the food and wine by components, think of the acidity in the tomatoes and balsamic vinegar. Using that as a primary concern, choose a dry white wine that also possesses good acidity, but is also herbal, such as a wine made from the Sauvignon Blanc grapes to create a flavor similarity.*

Suggestions:
Pouilly Fumé, Loire Valley (France) **$15-$25**
Sancerre, Loire Valley (France) **$15**
Cloudy Bay Sauvignon Blanc, Marlborough (New Zealand) **$16**
Barnard Griffin Fumé Blanc, Yakima Valley (Washington State) **$14**
Estancia Sauvignon Blanc, Monterey County (California) **$10**

2) *If you're going to match the food and wine by flavors, think of the strong flavor of the rosemary. Choose a spicy dry red wine that possesses good fruits, but has fairly good acidity.*

Suggestions:
Rosemount Shiraz, Hunter Valley, New South Wales (Australia) **$11**
Côtes du Rhône Villages, Rhône Valley (France) **$10**
Salice Salentino, Apula (Italy) **$10**
Booney Doon Le Cigare Volant (California) **$13**
Gundlach Bunschu Zinfandel, Sonoma (California) **$21**
Ferrari Corona Siena, Sonoma (California) **$25**
Rosenblum Petite Syrah, Napa (California) **$15**

Zuccotto alla Ricotta

ITALIAN LADYFINGER DOME FILLED WITH CREAM AND NUTS

Wine Criteria:
Try a young botrytized or late harvest white wine with this dish.

Suggestions:
Riesling Vendage Tardive, Alsace (France) **$35-$60**

Château Doisy-Daene, Bordeaux (France) **$30**

Tokaj Aszu "4 Puttonyos." Tokaj-Hegylia (Hungary) **$17**

Piesporter Goldtropfchen Riesling Auslese, Mosel-Saar Ruwer (Germany) **$22**

Maculan Torcolato, Veneto (Italy) **$65**

Far Niente Dolce, Napa Valley (California) **$60**

Joseph Phelps Delice, Napa Valley (California) **$16**

The Recipes

Fresh Mozzarella Balls with Pesto

If you've never tasted fresh mozzarella, you're in for a real treat... it has a creamy delicate flavor. Here we use the small bite-size mozzarella balls called "bocconcini". Roll the bocconcini in a fresh pesto sauce for an easy and delicious appetizer.

8 OUNCES BITE-SIZE FRESH MOZZARELLA BALLS A.K.A. "BOCCONCINI" *

Available at specialty grocers or an Italian delicatessen.

Pesto Sauce

1 CUP FRESH BASIL LEAVES

1 SMALL CLOVE GARLIC, MINCED

1/4 CUP FRESHLY GRATED PARMESAN OR PARMIGIANO REGGIANO CHEESE

1/3 CUP OLIVE OIL

1 TABLESPOON LEMON JUICE

1/4 CUP PINE NUTS

1/2 TEASPOON SALT

Wash and dry basil leaves, remove stems. Put all ingredients for pesto sauce (except the oil and lemon juice) in a food processor and blend for 5-8 seconds, until smooth. Scrap the sides of the bowl. Add oil and lemon juice and blend. Roll mozzarella balls in pesto sauce when ready to serve.

Garnish: Fresh basil leaves on plate.

Vegetable Lasagna

Another of my favorite recipes for which I'm famous. Once you've tasted how light the homemade noodles make this dish, you will never be able to eat store-bought lasagna noodles again. Get all the ingredients ahead and prepare this dish with your lover on a day when you have time to play in the kitchen!

Homemade Pasta Dough

2 CUPS UNBLEACHED FLOUR

2 WHOLE EGGS

1 TEASPOON SALT

1 TABLESPOON WATER, IF NEEDED *

In a food processor, insert metal blade. Add egg and salt and blend for 10 seconds. Then add flour quickly through the feed tube. Continue blending until mixture forms a ball (5-10 seconds until the machine slows down or stops). *If the dough is too dry add water; if too soft, add flour and knead into dough.* Wrap the dough in plastic wrap, let stand in a cool place for 45 minutes to 1 hour.

While the dough is resting, prepare tomato sauce and fillings.

Tomato Sauce

1-16 OUNCE CAN ITALIAN PLUM TOMATOES, DRAINED AND CHOPPED FINE

1 CLOVE GARLIC, CHOPPED

6 FRESH BASIL LEAVES, CHOPPED

2 TABLESPOONS OLIVE OIL

1/2 TEASPOON SALT

PEPPER TO TASTE

In a medium saucepan, over medium high heat, sauté garlic until golden, then add tomatoes, salt, pepper and basil. Simmer for 20 minutes.

Ricotta Cheese Filling

1 POUND RICOTTA CHEESE

¼ CUP MILK

PINCH NUTMEG, FRESHLY GRATED

1 TEASPOON SALT AND PEPPER TO TASTE

Mix ricotta cheese in mixing bowl; add milk, salt, pepper and nutmeg. Stir thoroughly. Set aside.

Vegetable Filling

2 MEDIUM ZUCCHINI, JULIENNED

1 RED BELL PEPPER, SLICED THIN

2 CARROTS, JULIENNED

2 TABLESPOONS OLIVE OIL

2 CLOVES GARLIC

1 BAG SPINACH CLEANED, BLANCHED AND DRAINED

1 CUP FRESH WHITE BUTTON MUSHROOMS, SLICED THIN

1 CUP MOZZARELLA CHEESE, SHREDDED

½ CUP FRESHLY GRATED PARMIGIANO REGGIANO OR PARMESAN CHEESE

SALT AND PEPPER TO TASTE

Note: The vegetable lasagna can be made with any of your favorite vegetables.

In a large frying pan, heat oil over medium high heat. Sauté garlic and onions until golden, then add mushrooms and sauté for another 2-3 minutes. Add red peppers, cook for 5 minutes. Add zucchini and sauté another 2-3 minutes longer. Salt to taste. Remove vegetables from pan and set aside.

After removing stems from spinach, quickly rinse in cold water. Place spinach leaves in your skillet, over medium heat, with no oil. Cover and cook 1-2 minutes until the spinach wilts. Remove spinach from pan and let cool. Then squeeze out excess water and chop. Heat oil and garlic over medium high heat until garlic is golden. Add chopped spinach and sauté another 1-2 minutes. Salt, pepper and sprinkle with a pinch of nutmeg. Set aside. Let cool.

To Finish Making the Lasagna Noodles
3 QUARTS SALTED WATER TO COOK NOODLES

When you unwrap pasta dough, it will seem more moist than it did originally. Do not add any more flour. Dust your hands with flour and knead dough for 1 minute. Divide dough into 4 parts. Flatten each piece, with palm of your hand.

Roll out dough using a hand-cranked pasta machine. Set rollers of pasta maker at the maximum opening. Run dough through 3 or 4 times, folding and turning it each time you feed it through. Then close the opening one notch, and run the dough through once. Continue closing the opening one notch at a time and feed pasta ribbon through the rollers once each time until the lowest notch is reached. **See diagram #3 on page 66.** If dough becomes too sticky, dust with flour. Lay each pasta ribbon/lasagna noodle out on a clean cotton dish cloth, until ready to boil in boiling water.

Bring a large pot of water to boil. Add 1 tablespoon salt to boiling water. Prepare a bowl of clean ice water for dunking noodles after they have been cooked in boiling water. Gently drop each noodle one by one in salted boiling water and boil for approximately 30 seconds to 1 minute.

Gently remove lasagna noodle with a slotted spoon and place it in bowl of ice water for just a second. Quickly remove noodle from ice water and place it on a flat surface lined with a clean cotton dish cloth. When all noodles have been cooked, you are now ready to begin making the lasagna.

To Assemble Lasagna

FRESH BASIL LEAVES (FOR GARNISH)

Preheat oven to 350 degrees F. Place some tomato sauce in bottom of a square baking pan. Begin layering the lasagna noodles in the pan, (cut noodles to fit the size of the baking pan) alternating layers of cheese filling, vegetable filling and sauce.

Note: Reserve some vegetables to garnish top of lasagna.

Try this sequence:
- Lasagna noodles topped with ricotta cheese mixture.
- Another layer of lasagna noodles with zucchini, carrots, mushrooms, peppers, parmesan cheese, mozzarella, spinach and tomato sauce.
- Another layer of lasagna noodles, with spinach, mozzarella cheese and parmesan.
- Finish the top layer with lasagna noodles covered with tomato sauce.
- Decorate top of lasagna with pieces of cooked vegetables, making diagonal lines, or square. Sprinkle parmesan cheese between vegetable design.
- Cover lasagna with aluminum foil and bake for 35 minutes. Remove from the oven and let cool for 20 minutes. Slice and serve.

Garnish: Spoon extra tomato sauce on each plate, topping with a piece of lasagna and several fresh basil leaves.

Sautéed Chicken Breasts with Balsamic Vinegar and Fresh Rosemary

Like most Italian chicken dishes, this one is quick and uncomplicated with very few ingredients. The combination of balsamic vinegar and fresh rosemary is unforgettable.

4 CHICKEN BREAST HALVES (BONED AND SKINLESS)

2 TABLESPOONS FLOUR

3 SPRIGS FRESH ROSEMARY*

1 WHOLE CLOVE GARLIC

¼ CUP BALSAMIC VINEGAR

⅓ CUP CHICKEN STOCK

¼ CUP FRESH PLUM TOMATOES, CHOPPED FINE

SALT AND PEPPER TO TASTE

* We do not suggest substituting dried rosemary for this recipe, use fresh only..

Place each chicken breast in a plastic bag (or between 2 sheets of plastic wrap) and pound with the flat side of meat cleaver until thin. Salt and pepper each side of chicken breast, then flour.

Heat olive oil and garlic in frying pan, over medium high heat, until the garlic turns golden. Remove garlic and discard. Turn heat to high. When oil is very hot, add chicken breasts, sauté until golden brown on each side. *Be careful not to burn them, adjust the heat if necessary.* Add 1 sprig fresh rosemary, balsamic vinegar, chicken stock, and chopped tomatoes. Simmer for 3-4 minutes.

Garnish: Fresh rosemary sprig on each plate.

Zuccotto alla Ricotta

Pastry shops in Rome and Florence are filled with all types of Zuccotto. Italians love this dessert as much or more than the classic Tiramisù. Although it is usually made with Italian sponge cake, I have devised an easier version using store-bought Italian ladyfingers or store-bought poundcake. It is partially frozen for a bit of crunch. Try it… you won't be disappointed. Prepare the day before to save time.

16 ITALIAN LADYFINGERS, OR POUND CAKE, STORE-BOUGHT

3/4 CUP WHOLE MILK RICOTTA CHEESE

1 CUP FRESHLY WHIPPED CREAM

1/2 CUP CONFECTIONERS SUGAR

1 TABLESPOON HAZELNUTS, CHOPPED FINE

1 TABLESPOON PINE NUTS, CHOPPED FINE

1 TABLESPOON PISTACHIO NUTS, CHOPPED FINE

1 TABLESPOON ALMONDS TOASTED , CHOPPED FINE

2 TABLESPOONS MINIATURE CHOCOLATE CHIPS

1 TEASPOON CANDIED ORANGE PEEL

1/2 CUP ESPRESSO

2 TABLESPOONS GRAND MARNIER

Line a small bowl, 6-7" diameter by 3-4" high, with a large enough piece of plastic wrap to cover the inside of the bowl and to fold over the top once the bowl has been filled. Prepare espresso, add Grand Marnier and let cool slightly. Using a pastry brush, lightly brush espresso and Grand Marnier on one side of ladyfingers or one side of poundcake slice. Line bowl with ladyfingers, or poundcake, starting at the bottom, then the sides, cutting them to fit. Assemble them as close together as possible, making a ladyfinger bowl.

In another bowl, mix ricotta cheese, $1/4$ cup confectioners sugar, nuts, chocolate chips and candied orange peel. Meanwhile, whip cream and $1/4$ cup confectioners sugar until stiff. Fold cream into ricotta mixture. Spoon this mixture into ladyfinger bowl. Level mixture with back of spoon. Fold plastic wrap over top and refrigerate for at least 6 hours, or overnight. Place in freezer the last hour before serving.

At serving time, lift plastic wrap off of top, turn bowl upside down onto a round serving plate releasing the zuccotto onto the plate. Slice into pie shaped pieces.

Garnish: Sprinkle more confectioners sugar and serve at once.

Stuffed Eggplant Roll-Ups
EGGPLANT SLICES STUFFED WITH A RICOTTA CHEESE MIXTURE,
ROLLED AND TOPPED WITH HOMEMADE TOMATO SAUCE

Spaghettini Marinara
THIN PASTA NOODLES TOPPED WITH HOMEMADE TOMATO SAUCE

Tilapia Pizzaiola
BROILED WITH TOMATOES, GARLIC, OREGANO, BREAD CRUMBS AND OIL

Norma's Cannoli
ITALIAN PASTRY FILLED WITH CREAM AND CHOCOLATE CHIPS

For A Little Romance:

Put a table cloth on the living room floor with lots of pillows, so you can relax between courses. Prepare a small picnic basket painted white. Fill it full of potted or fresh cut flowers to use as a centerpiece. Light lots of vanilla scented candles all around the room, and don't forget the music.

Let's Talk Wines For This Menu

Stuffed Eggplant Roll-Ups
STUFFED WITH RICOTTA CHEESE MIXTURES AND
TOPPED WITH TOMATO SAUCE AND MOZZARELLA

Wine Criteria:
The key element in this dish is the acidity, both in the tomato sauce and the ricotta cheese, as well as in the smoky bitter flavor of the eggplant. Therefore, choose a grassy, oaky style dry white wine from a cool climate.

Suggestions:
❤ Pouilly Fumé, Loire Valley, (France) **$15**
Robert Mondavi Sauvignon Blanc "SLD" Napa, (California) **$19**

Or choose a medium-bodied red from a warm climate that possesses young, spicy fruits, such as California Zinfandel.

Suggestions:
Gundlach Bunschu Zinfandel, Sonoma (California) **$22**
Ravenswood Zinfandel, Sonoma, (California) **$15**
Backsberg Pinotage, Paarl Wo (South Africa) **$10**
Côtes du Rhône Village, Rhône Valley (France) **$10**
Chianti Classico, Tuscany (Italy) **$12 -$15**

❤ *Romantic Match/See Wine Glossary*

Spaghettini Marinara
THIN PASTA NOODLES TOPPED WITH HOMEMADE TOMATO SAUCE

Wine Criteria:
Choose a white wine similar to the style described in the first course, or a young light red from a cooler climate, such as a California Zinfandel or a Washington State Merlot.

Suggestions:
Beringer Zinfandel, Napa Valley (California) **$13**
Ravenswood Zinfandel, Sonoma (California) **$15**
Château Ste. Michelle Merlot, Columbia Valley (Washington State) **$15**

Tilapia (or White Fish) Pizzaiola
BROILED WITH FRESH TOMATOES, GARLIC, OREGANO, BREAD CRUMBS AND OIL

Suggestions:
You can continue with a white wine from the styles described in the first and second course.

Norma's Cannoli
ITALIAN PASTRY FILLED WITH CREAM AND CHOCOLATE CHIPS

Wine Criteria:
Choose a botrytized sweet white wine such as a Sauterne or a Barsac from France.

Suggestions:
Château Climent, Barsac (France) **$35-$50**
B & G Sauternes, Bordeaux (France) **$20**
Kracher Muskat Ottonel Beernauslese, Neusiedler See (Austria) **$30**

Or choose a sweet to medium-sweet Sparkling Wine or Champagne.
Suggestions:
Martini & Rossi Asti Spumante, Piedmont (Italy) **$10**
Vintage Schramsberg Crement, Napa Valley (California) **$22**
NV Veuve Clicquot Demi-Sec, Champagne (France) **$33**

Stuffed Eggplant Roll-Ups

Although we have listed this dish as an appetizer, it is hearty enough to be used as a first course. This recipe, depending on size of eggplant, will yield 5-6 roll-ups. Enjoy the extras for lunch the next day.

1 MEDIUM SIZE EGGPLANT, CUT INTO $1/2$" SLICES

$1/4$ TEASPOON SALT

Slice eggplant lengthwise into $1/2$ inch slices. Discard end slices that are mostly skin. Lay slices on a baking sheet and salt them. Let set for 30 minutes to 1 hour, allowing the bitter juices to seep out. Meanwhile, prepare tomato sauce and filling.

Tomato Sauce

1 TABLESPOON OLIVE OIL

1 CLOVE FRESH GARLIC, MINCED

1 - 8 OUNCE CAN PLUM TOMATOES, PEELED AND CRUSHED

$1/2$ TEASPOON SALT

5 FRESH BASIL LEAVES, MINCED

In a medium saucepan, heat 1 tablespoon olive oil and garlic until garlic is golden.
Crush tomatoes in a food processor for 5-10 seconds. Then add tomatoes, salt, pepper, and fresh basil to saucepan and simmer for 20 minutes.

Filling

1/2 POUND RICOTTA CHEESE, DRAIN IN A MESH STRAINER, IF NEEDED

1 WHOLE EGG OR 1 EGG WHITE

1 TEASPOON FRESH ITALIAN PARSLEY, CHOPPED FINE

1 TABLESPOON FRESHLY GRATED PARMIGIANO REGGIANO OR PARMESAN CHEESE

1 CLOVE GARLIC, CRUSHED

1/2 TEASPOON SALT

PEPPER TO TASTE

PINCH FRESHLY GRATED NUTMEG

Drain ricotta in a mesh strainer if too wet. Then mix all filling ingredients in a medium bowl. Set aside.

To Assemble and Prepare Roll-ups

1/4 CUP VEGETABLE OIL

3/4 CUP PLAIN BREAD CRUMBS

1/4 CUP FLOUR

1 LARGE EGG

6 SLICES MOZZARELLA CHEESE

2 TABLESPOONS FRESHLY GRATED PARMESAN CHEESE (FOR GARNISH)

FRESH BASIL LEAVES (FOR GARNISH)

Rinse eggplant in cold water and pat dry with a paper towel. Beat egg and 1 tablespoon milk together. Dip eggplant slices in egg mixture, then in bread crumbs. Push bread crumbs in with palm of your hand.

Preheat oven to 350 degrees F. Heat oil in a heavy skillet over high heat. When hot, fry breaded eggplant until golden brown on both sides. Drain on paper towels and let cool.

On a flat surface, lay out eggplant slices, place 1 tablespoon of ricotta mixture in the middle and roll lengthwise. Secure with toothpick, if necessary. Place roll-up in baking dish and top each one with a slice of mozzarella.

Bake in a preheated oven until cheese melts, about 10-15 minutes. Spoon tomato sauce on each serving plate. Place eggplant roll-up on top of sauce and add more sauce on top. Serve immediately.

Garnish: Fresh basil leaves.

Spaghettini Marinara

This marinara sauce is used for many recipes. Why not make up some extra and freeze it in small containers to use for different recipes?

Homemade Tomato Sauce a.k.a. "Marinara Sauce"

8 FRESH (RIPE) PLUM TOMATOES OR 1 - 16 OUNCE CAN ITALIAN PLUM TOMATOES, CHOPPED WITH JUICE

1 CLOVE GARLIC, MINCED

5 LEAVES FRESH BASIL, CHOPPED FINE

1/2 TEASPOON SALT

PEPPER TO TASTE

1 TABLESPOON OLIVE OIL

If using fresh tomatoes, par boil until skins break, remove skins and seeds. Chop fine by hand or use a food processor for 5 seconds. In a saucepan, heat oil and garlic, over medium high heat, until garlic is golden. Add tomatoes, salt and fresh basil. Simmer for 20 minutes.

Prepare Spaghettini

8 OUNCES STORE-BOUGHT SPAGHETTINI*

3 QUARTS WATER FOR COOKING PASTA

1 TEASPOON SALT

1 TABLESPOON PARMIGIANO REGGIANO OR PARMENSAN CHEESE,
FRESHLY GRATED (FOR GARNISH)

FRESH BASIL LEAVES (FOR GARNISH)

* Spaghettini is thin spaghetti noodles, also called capellini or angel hair.

In a large pot, bring 3 quarts of water to boil. Add salt. Cook spaghettini until *"al dente."* Test for doneness by tasting a single piece. Drain water, and return to pan. Quickly add marinara sauce and toss. Serve immediately in pasta bowls.

Garnish: Fresh grated parmesan cheese and fresh basil leaves.

Tilapia Pizzaiola

Also known as St. Peter's fish, tilapia has a wonderful mild, sweet flavor, tastier than white fish. Egyptian hieroglyphics dating from 2500 B.C. mention tilapia.

4 FILETS FRESH TILAPIA OR WHITE FISH

1 LARGE TOMATO, SLICED THIN

1 OUNCES PLAIN BREAD CRUMBS

1 CLOVE GARLIC, CRUSHED

2 TABLESPOONS OLIVE OIL

PINCH DRIED OREGANO

1 BAY LEAF

SALT AND PEPPER, TO TASTE

½ LEMON, SLICED (FOR GARNISH)

Salt fish on both sides. In a baking dish, place tilapia. Add sliced tomato, garlic, salt pepper, oregano, bay leaf and bread crumbs. Drizzle olive oil over top. Let marinate for 1 hour. Preheat broiler. Broil fish in the same baking dish as tomato slices for 10 minutes, or until top is golden brown. Remove bay leaf.

Garnish: Lemon slices.

Norma's Cannoli

You haven't lived until you have tasted one of these Italian treats.
The experience surpasses any written description.

Homemade Cannoli Shells

1 WHOLE EGG

¼ CUP COLD WATER

⅛ CUP SUGAR

1¼ CUP FLOUR

2 TABLESPOONS CRISCO SHORTENING

⅛ TEASPOON SALT

1 SMALL CINNAMON STICK, CRUSHED

½ SHOT WHISKEY

1 TABLESPOON ROASTED ALMONDS, CRUSHED

⅛ CUP CANOLA OIL, FOR FRYING

Note this recipe will yield about 8 cannoli.

In a large bowl, mix together egg, whiskey, water and sugar. Then add the rest of ingredients, except canola oil used for frying. Mix thoroughly. Knead dough on a lightly floured working surface until smooth and elastic, add more flour if needed.

Wrap dough in plastic wrap and put in the refrigerator for 1 hour.

Then roll dough out on a floured surface until it is about ⅛" thick. Cut out circles with a 3" or 4" cookie cutter, depending on the size cannoli you want. Roll a rolling pin over each circle to lengthen it slightly making an oval shape.

Wrap dough ovals around cannoli pipes, overlapping one end over the other. Moisten dough with a little water on your fingertips if ovals don't stick together. Heat canola oil in a heavy skillet, over medium high heat. Fry cannoli, a few at a time, in the preheated oil until they are golden brown on all sides. Remove cannoli from hot oil using metal tongs, and set aside on a paper towel to drain for one minute.

You must remove cannoli from the metal tubes before they cool and shrink, otherwise they will break. Remove cannoli from tube by holding the end of tube with the tongs. With a paper towel in the other hand, slide cannoli off tube.

Diagram #7

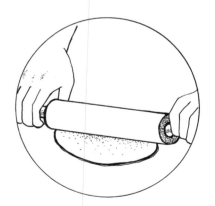

Italian Pastry Cream Filling

1¼ CUP COLD MILK

1 EGG YOLK

3 TABLESPOONS SUGAR

3 TABLESPOONS FLOUR

1 CINNAMON STICK

1 TEASPOON ORANGE AND LEMON PEEL (ZEST)

1 TABLESPOON SMALL CHOCOLATE CHIPS

2 TABLESPOONS POWDERED SUGAR (FOR GARNISH)

2 TABLESPOONS TOASTED ALMONDS, CRUSHED (FOR GARNISH)

Optional: Use ice cream or Ricotta filling (see recipe next page) in place of pastry cream.

In a saucepan, over medium heat, put cold milk, sugar, egg yolk and flour. Stir well, with a wire whisk, until flour is completely dissolved, and there are no lumps. Then add cinnamon stick, orange and lemon peel. Continue cooking over medium high heat, stirring constantly, until the mixture thickens. Scrape sides and bottom of pan to keep from sticking. Remove from heat and discard cinnamon stick, orange and lemon peels. Cover surface with plastic wrap and refrigerate until cold. Stir in chocolate chips. About one hour before serving, fill cannoli shells with pastry cream filling using a pastry bag fitted with a 1/2 inch plain tube or you can use a small spoon.

Garnish: Sprinkle both ends of the cream, inside the cannoli, with crushed almonds. Dust top of the cannoli with powdered sugar.

Optional Ricotta Filling

½ POUND FRESH RICOTTA CHEESE

4 TABLESPOONS POWDERED SUGAR

1 TABLESPOON CHOCOLATE CHIPS

1 TABLESPOON GRAND MARNIER

1 TABLESPOON TOASTED ALMONDS, CHOPPED

Beat ricotta, sugar, and Grand Marnier until very light, using a mixer at medium speed. Then, stir in chocolate chips. About one hour before serving, fill shells with ricotta filling, using a pastry bag fitted with a ½ inch plain tube, or use a small spoon.

Garnish: Sprinkle both ends of the cream, inside the cannoli, with crushed almonds, and dust top of cannoli with powdered sugar.

The Menu

Fried Baby Artichokes
YOUNG TENDER ARTICHOKES DIPPED IN EGG BATTER, FRIED AND SERVED WITH LEMON

Seafood Pasta
FRESH SHRIMP, CLAMS, MUSSELS AND LOBSTER IN A WHITE WINE SAUCE

Grilled Veal Chops
TOPPED WITH WILD MUSHROOM SAUCE

Espresso Granita
FROZEN ESPRESSO SHAVINGS TOPPED WITH FRESHLY WHIPPED CREAM

For A Little Romance:

Plan an Italian theme dinner. Start with a red and white checkered table cloth, big white cloth napkins, candles in empty Chianti wine bottles (the ones from Italy with jute around the bottle.) And, don't forget Pavarotti playing while you eat your pasta. Write this Italian toast on a piece of paper and say it each time you raise your glass. **Amore mio, chin, chin. Ti amo!** Pronounced: (Ahmoray meeo, chin, chin, tee ahmo.) Translation: My love, here's to you. I love you!

Let's Talk Wines For This Menu

Fried Baby Artichokes
YOUNG TENDER ARTICHOKES DIPPED IN EGG, FRIED AND SERVED WITH LEMON

Wine Criteria:
Artichokes are difficult to match with wine, as there is a chemical in artichokes that makes the wine have an unpleasant sweet aftertaste. Therefore, serve a white wine that is extremely dry and acidic to compensate for the extra sweetness.

Suggestions:
Robert Mondavi Sauvignon Blanc, Napa Valley (California) **$14**
Pouilly Fumé, Loire Valley (France) **$15-$20**
Chablis AC, Burgundy (France) **$19-$24**
Muscadet de Sevre-et-Maine, Loire Valley (France) **$8**

Or you may choose a young, dry red wine that has fairly good fruits, acidity, and is low in tannins.
Suggestion:
Barbera d'Alba, Piedmont (Italy) **$10-$15**

Another choice would be a bone-dry, non-vintage Champagne, since the sweet after-taste created when matched with the artichokes would seem like an improvement to the Champagne. What a way to turn something that might appear unpleasant to one's palate into a pleasant experience!
Suggestion:
NV Laurent-Perrier Brut, Champagne (France) **$35**

Grilled Veal Chops
TOPPED WITH WILD MUSHROOM SAUCE

Wine Criteria:

In this dish you are dealing with grilled smoky flavors of veal and the earthy texture of the mushroom sauce. Therefore, I would match this dish based on contrast of flavors and similar texture. This means choosing a red wine that possesses good fruits (to contrast the smoky flavor, and a velvety texture to match the mushroom sauce texture), such as a California or Oregon Pinot Noirs from a good producer. Or serve a full-bodied, oaky, dry red wine from a cool climate. For example, a red Bordeaux which offers a great variety at all prices. My advice is this, the more you spend on the veal, the more you should spend on the wine.

Suggestions:

Domaine Drouhin Pinot Noir, Willamette Valley (Oregon) **$40**

Sanford Barrel Select "Sanford & Benedict" Pinot Noir, Santa Barbara (California) **$40**

Saintsbury Pinot Noir, Carneros (California) **$16**

Gevrey-Chambertin, Burgundy (France) **$25-$50**

Château Bel Air, Bordeaux (France) **$12**

Château Haut Brion, Bordeaux (France) **$75-$200** *depending on the vintage*

Clos du Val Cabernet Sauvignon, Napa Valley (California) **$15**

Columbia Crest Cabernet Sauvignon, Columbia Valley (Washington State) **$12**

Penfolds Bin 707 Cabernet Sauvignon, South-Australia (Australia) **$40**

Seafood Fettucine

FRESH SHRIMP, CLAMS, MUSSELS AND LOBSTER IN A WHITE WINE SAUCE

Wine Criteria:
Choose an aromatic, grassy dry white wine that is full-flavored, full-bodied, and from a young vintage, thus yielding a higher acidity.

Suggestions:
Robert Mondavi Sauvignon Blanc "SLD", Napa Valley, (California) **$19**
Avignonesi Il Vignola, Tuscany, (Italy) **$25**
Cloudy Bay Sauvignon Blanc, Marlborough, (New Zealand) **$15**
Château Lynch Bages Blanc, Bordeaux, (France) **$30**
Muscadet de Sevre-et-Maine, Loire Valley, (France) **$8** *budget choice*
(Although the budget choice is a light style wine, the acidity in this style of wine would stand up to the dish.)

Espresso Granita

FROZEN ESPRESSO SHAVINGS LAYERED BETWEEN FRESHLY WHIPPED CREAM

Wine Criteria:
My best advice is to enjoy this frozen cream dessert and have a glass of wine later. But if you insist on serving wine with this dessert, I find a full-bodied, sweet style sherry works best.

Suggestion:
Lustau Pedro Ximenez Golden Brown & Sweet Sherry (Spain) **$13**
Or my budget choices would be:
Evian Water (France)
St. Pelligrino (Italy)

Fried Baby Artichokes

The secret to this recipe is to use young, tender baby artichokes, that are very green and fresh. These little ones are almost entirely edible.

6 BABY ARTICHOKES

$1/4$ CUP FLOUR, UNBLEACHED

1 WHOLE EGG, BEATEN

2 TABLESPOONS MILK

$1/4$ CUP FRESH LEMON JUICE

$1/4$ CUP OLIVE OIL

$1 1/2$ TEASPOONS SALT

To Prepare Artichokes

3 QUARTS BOILING WATER, SALTED

Fill a medium bowl with cold water and lemon juice. Bend leaves of artichokes backwards until they break off as close to the base as possible. Cut artichokes in half, leaving the stem intact, trimming $1/8$" off the bottom of stem. Then place artichoke halves in a bowl of cold water and lemon to prevent them from turning brown. (Do not use an aluminum bowl or pan, as it will turn the artichokes black.) Bring 3 quarts of water to boil. Add 1 teaspoon salt to water, and cook artichokes for 10 minutes. Drain and let cool.

Flour the artichokes. Mix egg, milk and $1/2$ teaspoon salt together, then dip artichokes into mixture. In a skillet, heat olive oil over medium high heat. Fry artichokes until golden brown on both sides.

Garnish: Serve with lemon wedges.

Diagram #8

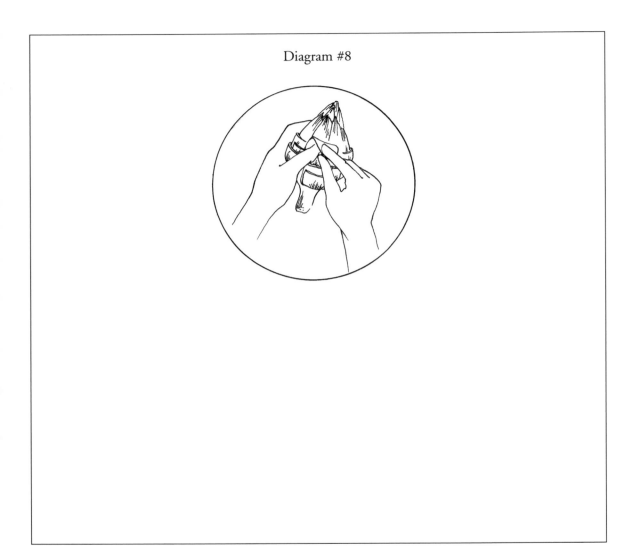

Seafood Fettucine

This spectacular pasta dish "pictured on our cover" is one that will have the seafood lover on their knees begging more!

1/2 POUND FRESH JUMBO SHRIMP, PEELED AND DEVEINED (LEAVE THE TAILS)

12 FRESH MUSSELS, SCRUBBED

12 FRESH CLAMS, SCRUBBED

1- 4 OZ. FROZEN LOBSTER TAIL

4 TABLESPOONS OLIVE OIL

2 CLOVES GARLIC, CHOPPED

3 ANCHOVY FILETS

1 CUP FRESH TOMATOES OR AN 8 OZ. CAN OF TOMATOES

$1/3$ CUP WHITE WINE

1 TEASPOON SALT

1 RED HOT PEPPER OR 1/8 TEASPOON RED PEPPER FLAKES

1 TABLESPOON FRESH ITALIAN FLAT PARSLEY, CHOPPED

8 OZ. FETTUCINE NOODLES - COOK AS DIRECTED

Scrub and rinse clams and mussels. Remove the beard from mussels, then soak clams and mussels in a bowl of cold water for 1 hour. Thaw lobster tail in cold water for $1/2$ hour. Peel and devein shrimp, leaving the tails attached.

In a large skillet, heat oil and garlic over medium high heat until garlic is golden. Add anchovy filets and hot pepper. Mash anchovies with wooden spoon and stir. Drain mussels and clams, then add to hot oil. Cover and cook over high heat (5-10 minutes) until the shells open. Discard any that do not open. Add shrimp and lobster tail. Cook uncovered another 5 minutes. Add wine, then tomatoes, and cook another five minutes. Salt to taste and add chopped parsley. Remove lobster tail from the shell and cut into large cubes.

Meanwhile, cook fettucine noodles in 3 quarts salted boiling water until it is *"al dente."* Drain. Place in large pasta bowl for mixing. Remove all cooked seafood from juice in pan. Pour half the juice over fettucine noodles and toss. Dish up in large individual serving bowls. Arrange clams, mussels, shrimp and lobster chunks on top of the pasta. Leave clams and mussels in their shells.

Garnish: Freshly chopped Italian parsley.

Note: *At each place setting, be sure to set out a pretty bowl to discard the empty clam and mussel shells. Also provide finger bowls with warm water and a lemon slice for cleaning hands, along with a crisp white cloth to dry hands.*

Grilled Veal Chops with Wild Mushrooms

This recipe for thick, juicy veal chops is very easy to prepare, and is truly unforgettable.

2 VEAL CHOPS 1½" THICK

SALT AND PEPPER – TO TASTE

Salt and pepper both sides of veal chops. Grill over hot coals for 10 minutes on each side.

Wild Mushroom Sauce

1½ CUPS ASSORTED FRESH MUSHROOMS IN SEASON, SLICED THIN

1 LARGE CLOVE GARLIC, CHOPPED FINE

2 MEDIUM SHALLOTS, CHOPPED LENGTHWISE

½ TEASPOON SALT

PEPPER, TO TASTE

2 TABLESPOONS OLIVE OIL

¼ CUP WHITE WINE

1 TABLESPOON CREAM

1 SMALL FRESH TOMATO, CHOPPED FINE

FRESH ITALIAN PARSLEY (FOR GARNISH)

Wipe or brush fresh mushrooms clean. Cut mushrooms into thin lengthwise slices. Heat oil and garlic in a heavy skillet, over medium high heat. Add shallots and sauté until golden. Add mushrooms, and cook for a few more minutes. Then, add wine and let evaporate. Add salt, pepper and cream. Quickly toss in fresh tomato. Stir gently. Cook for 5 more minutes. Remove from heat and spoon over veal chops.

Garnish: Sprig of Italian parsley.

Espresso Granita

Granita is one of the most refreshing ways to bring a meal
to a close, especially for the coffee lover.

1 CUP FRESHLY BREWED STRONG ITALIAN ESPRESSO

¼ CUP SUGAR

1 CUP FRESHLY WHIPPED CREAM

2 TABLESPOONS POWDERED SUGAR

1 SPRIG FRESH MINT (FOR GARNISH)

1 TEASPOON CHOCOLATE SHAVINGS (FOR GARNISH)

Brew espresso, add sugar, stir until dissolved. Let cool. Pour coffee mixture into a small metal cake pan. Place in freezer for about 45 minutes. Remove from freezer and stir, breaking ice crystals. Return to freezer and repeat procedure, stirring or scraping the ice with a fork at 15 minute intervals, until an icy slush is formed. It takes about two hours to reach a proper slushy consistency.

Note: If granita becomes too hard in freezer, grind it in a blender before serving. If you don't plan to serve the granita right away, store in a plastic container in freezer for up to 2 hours.

To serve, whip cream and sugar together until stiff. Break up and stir ice crystals one more time. Serve in a small parfait glass or small wine glass, alternating layers of freshly whipped cream with the frozen espresso. Finish with an espresso layer. Spoon a dollop of whipped cream over top.

Garnish: Chocolate shavings and fresh mint.

The Menu

Bruschetta
HEARTY BREAD TOPPED WITH ROASTED RED AND YELLOW PEPPERS

Spaghetti and Meatballs
TRADITIONAL ITALIAN MEATBALLS MADE WITH VEAL, BREAD CRUMBS AND MILK

Chicken Florentine
CHICKEN BREASTS TOPPED WITH SPINACH AND MOZZARELLA

Italian Kisses
RICH CHOCOLATE AND HAZELNUT COOKIE KISSES

A Little Romance:

Routine and predictability lead to boredom in a relationship. Try serving the spaghetti and meatballs without silverware. Only use your fingers to eat! Start by feeding each other the first few bites. This is called "courtship feeding" or "food sharing," a primeval ritual. Finger licking is allowed! Be sure to use oversize bibs. Pretty dish towels work great! Have finger bowls at each place setting with warm lemon water and a flower floating on top. These are the kind of unexpected moments that will keep your lover looking forward to spending time alone with you.

Let's Talk Wines For This Menu

Bruschetta
HEARTY BREAD TOASTED AND TOPPED WITH
ROASTED RED AND YELLOW PEPPERS

Wine Criteria:
The key component in this dish is the roasted peppers, which require an aromatic, grassy, dry style white wine that is unoaked. A good choice would be a Sauvignon Blanc from California or a Bordeaux from France. Or even, a Vouvray, which is made from the Chenin Blanc grapes, would work well.

Suggestions:
Château Moncontour Vouvray, Loire Valley (France) **$10**
Château Millet, Bordeaux (France) **$14**
Kenwood Sauvignon Blanc, Sonoma (California) **$10**
Chalone Chenin Blanc, Monterey (California) **$15**
Château Ste. Michelle Sauvignon Blanc, Columbia Valley (Washington State) **$9**
Gamla Sauvignon Blanc, Golan Heights (Israel) **$13**
Boschendal Sauvignon Blanc, Stellenbosch (South Africa) **$13**

Spaghetti and Meatballs
TRADITIONAL ITALIAN MEATBALLS WITH VEAL, BREAD CRUMBS AND MILK

Wine Criteria:
Choose a medium-bodied dry red wine from a warm climate, that possesses good fruits and acidity.

Suggestions:
Sanford Pinot Noir, Central Coast (California) **$20**
Atlas Peak Sangiovesse, Napa Valley (California) **$15**
Beaulieu Vineyard Beautour Cabernet Sauvignon, Napa Valley (California) **$10**
Wolf Blass "Yellow Label" Cabernet Sauvignon, South Australia (Australia) **$10**
Côtes du Rhône Village, Rhône Valley (France) **$10**
Ducale Chianti Classico Riserva, Tuscany (Italy) **$15**
Argiano Rosso di Montalcino, Tuscany (Italy) **$17**

Chicken Florentine
CHICKEN BREASTS TOPPED WITH SPINACH AND MOZZARELLA CHEESE

Wine Criteria:
Choose an unoaked, fruity, dry white wine from a cool climate, as these wines possess good acidity that is needed to stand up to the spinach.

Suggestions:
Pinot Blanc, Alsace (France) **$10-$15**
Muscadet de Sevre-et-Maine, Loire Valley (France) **$8**
Fourchaume Chablis AC, Burgundy (France) **$24**
Chalone Chenin Blanc, Monterey (California) **$15**
Calera Viognier, Mt. Harlan (California) **$35**
Château Musar Blanc, Ghazir (Lebanon) **$12**

Italian Kisses
RICH CHOCOLATE AND HAZELNUT COOKIE KISSES

Wine Criteria:
Chocolate is difficult to match with dessert wines, therefore your options are going to be limited. I find that a fortified style wine such as a "vintage port" or a "vintage character port" is the best choice. However, you may select a young, botrytized, sweet wine, such as a young vigorous Sauternes or a "Vindage Tardive" style wine from Alsace.

Suggestions:
Château Climents, Bordeaux, (France) **$45**
Tokay Pinot Gris "Vindage Tardive", Alsace (France) **$35-$60**
Grahams "Six Grapes" Porto, Duoro (Portugal) **$18**
Evian Water (France) **$2** *budget choice*

Bruschetta with Roasted Peppers

Easy and delicious, these peppers have a delicate sweet taste that cannot be
duplicated. Serve over hearty French or Italian bread, lightly toasted.

$1/2$ BAGUETTE HEARTY FRENCH OR ITALIAN BREAD, SLICED $1/2$" THICK

1 MEDIUM RED PEPPER, ROASTED

1 MEDIUM YELLOW PEPPER, ROASTED

$1/8$ CUP OLIVE OIL

SALT AND PEPPER, TO TASTE

6 LEAVES FRESH BASIL, CHOPPED

$1/2$ TEASPOON CAPERS

1 SMALL CLOVE GARLIC, CRUSHED

Grill or broil peppers on a foil-lined baking sheet until skins are charred on all sides.
Place peppers in a plastic bag until cool enough to handle. Peel off charred skin. Remove
seeds and stem. Cut peppers into strips $3/4$" thick. Place peppers on a plate, top with crushed
garlic, olive oil, salt and pepper and let marinate for at least one hour. Just before serving, toast
bread on both sides under broiler until golden brown. Place peppers on top of toast and serve.
Garnish: Sprinkle capers on top of peppers.

Spaghetti and Meatballs alla Modesta

This conventional Italian dish will win rave reviews, especially from men, for the best meatballs they've ever tasted! You've got to try them.

Tomato Sauce

1-16 OZ. CAN OF ITALIAN PLUM TOMATOES, PEELED AND CHOPPED

2 WHOLE CLOVES GARLIC

2 TABLESPOONS OLIVE OIL

1 TEASPOON SALT

PEPPER TO TASTE

8 LEAVES FRESH BASIL, CHOPPED

In a heavy skillet, over medium, heat oil and garlic cloves until golden.
Add tomatoes, salt and pepper and fresh basil leaves. Simmer for 20 minutes. While the sauce is simmering, make your meatballs.

Meatballs

1 POUND GROUND VEAL OR GROUND TURKEY BREAST

2 CLOVES GARLIC, MINCED

1 SMALL ONION MINCED

1/4 CUP FRESHLY GRATED PARMESAN CHEESE, PLUS 2 TABLESPOONS FOR GARNISH

1 CUP PLAIN BREAD CRUMBS OR STALE BREAD SOAKED IN MILK

1 TABLESPOON FRESH PARSLEY, MINCED

Meatballs (continued)

1/2 CUP MILK

1 EGG WHITE

1 TEASPOON SALT

PEPPER TO TASTE

2 TABLESPOONS FRESH TOMATO SAUCE (SEE RECIPE PAGE 129)

In a medium size bowl, add all ingredients except the meat. Mix thoroughly. Then add ground veal or ground turkey breast. Mix all ingredients together. The mixture should be moist, if too dry, add a little more milk. Roll into medium size meatballs. Drop them into tomato sauce and cook over low heat for approximately 45 minutes. Remove garlic cloves before serving.

Pasta

8 OUNCES SPAGHETTI, COOK AL DENTE

3 QUARTS WATER

1 TEASPOON SALT.

2 TABLESPOONS FRESHLY GRATED PARMIGIANO REGGIANO OR
PARMESAN CHEESE (FOR GARNISH)

Bring water to boil. Add salt. Add pasta and cook *"al dente."* Remember it is better to undercook pasta than overcook it. Drain pasta. Return pasta to pan it was cooked in, and stir in some of the tomato sauce and meatballs. Toss gently. Serve in pasta bowls, and put a few more meatballs on the top.

Garnish: Freshly grated parmesan cheese.

Chicken Florentine

Another easy, delicious, and colorful dish, topped with spinach and mozzarella cheese.

1 CUP FRESH SPINACH LEAVES, WASHED AND STEMMED

1 TABLESPOON OLIVE OIL

1 WHOLE CLOVE GARLIC

SALT TO TASTE

PINCH FRESHLY GRATED NUTMEG

Rinse spinach, pat dry. Place spinach in a covered pan for a couple minutes until it wilts. Let cool. Squeeze out excess water and chop. Heat 1 tablespoon of olive oil and 1 clove of garlic until golden. Add spinach, salt, and sauté for 1 minute. Remove from heat. Add nutmeg. Set aside to use on top of chicken breasts. Blot excess liquid from spinach with a paper towel.

2 WHOLE CHICKEN BREASTS (BONED AND SKINLESS)

3 TABLESPOONS FLOUR

3 TABLESPOONS OLIVE OIL

1 CLOVE GARLIC

1/4 CUP DRY WHITE WINE

1/3 CUP CHICKEN STOCK

1 FRESH PLUM TOMATO, CHOPPED

SALT AND PEPPER TO TASTE

2 SLICES MOZZARELLA CHEESE

1 OUNCE FRESHLY GRATED PARMESAN CHEESE

FRESH ITALIAN PARSLEY (FOR GARNISH)

Cut chicken breasts in half, this will yield 4 pieces. Place each breast between 2 layers of plastic wrap (or in a large plastic bag) on a cutting board, pound each breast until thin using the flat side of a meat cleaver. Salt and pepper each side of breasts, then dust generously with flour.

Heat oil and garlic, in a large frying pan, over medium high heat until garlic is golden. Remove garlic and turn heat to high. Place chicken breasts in hot oil and brown on both sides. *Use a splatter screen if desired.* Add white wine, simmer for a few minutes until wine evaporates. Then add half the chicken stock. Add diced tomato and stir in sauce. Add more chicken stock if sauce has cooked down too much. Place a mound of spinach in center of chicken breast. Add a slice of Mozzarella cheese cupped or coned over spinach mound. Lower heat and cover pan for 1 minute until cheese melts.

Garnish: Spoon sauce on serving plate. Sprinkle each chicken breast with freshly grated parmesan cheese and add a sprig of parsley.

Italian Kisses

Everything love means can be expressed in a kiss. Show your love with a kiss, and your affection with one (or two) of these delectable Italian kisses. Worth every sinful bite! The Italian word for kiss is "Baci," pronounced Bahchee.

1 LARGE EGG WHITE

1/2 CUP SUGAR

3 TABLESPOONS COCOA, SIFTED

3/4 CUP FINELY GROUND HAZELNUTS (ALMONDS MAY BE SUBSTITUTED)

1/4 TEASPOON SHORTENING

2 OUNCES SEMISWEET CHOCOLATE, MELTED OR

TRY USING 2 OUNCES OF NUTELLA *

This recipe will yield about 8 kisses.
* *Nutella is a brand name of an Italian chocolate spread made of chocolate and hazelnuts. It is available in many specialty grocery stores.*

Preheat oven to 325 degrees F. Place egg white in a clean bowl. Beat on high speed with an electric mixer until egg white is stiff. Add sugar slowly and continue beating until egg white is very thick, about 3 minutes. Beat in cocoa until combined. Then stir in hazelnuts and mix until completely blended. The batter should be very thick and sticky.

Line a baking sheet with parchment. Dampen hands and shape 1 teaspoonful of dough into a 1-inch ball and place on baking sheet. Space balls about 2 inches apart. Bake until cookies are slightly cracked, about 15 minutes. Let cool on baking sheet for several minutes, then transfer to a rack and cool completely.

Melt chocolate in a saucepan over medium heat. When melted, remove from heat and stir in shortening. Spoon about 1/2 teaspoon of melted chocolate and shortening onto flat side of cooled cookie. Then attach flat side of another cookie to the first cookie as if they are kissing….get it! Press the two cookies together gently so the chocolate oozes out slightly. Return cookie to rack and let chocolate harden. Repeat with remaining cookies.

Garnish: Sprinkle a little cocoa powder on each serving plate and an Italian kiss, accompanied by a passionate *"10-second kiss!"*

Diagram #9

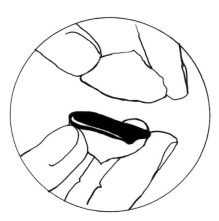

Portobello Napoleon

GRILLED PORTOBELLO MUSHROOMS, EGGPLANTS, RED PEPPERS, AND CHEESE

Fresh Vegetable Pasta

FRESH GARDEN VEGETABLES IN A LIGHT CREAM SAUCE

Grilled Shrimps

SERVED WITH A DIJON MUSTARD AND HONEY SAUCE

Grilled Banana & Pineapple

TOPPED WITH HONEY, BROWN SUGAR AND NUTS

For A Little Romance:

In your backyard (patio, deck or balcony) set up a table under your favorite tree, plant or umbrella. Cover the table with citronella candles floating in champagne or wine glasses. Wrap white Christmas tree lights around the plant, tree or umbrella pole. Hang ribbons with colorful hearts cut out and taped to the ends from the plant, tree or inside of the umbrella. Use napkins and a tablecloth to match the ribbons. Plan this meal at sunset.

Let's Talk Wines For This Menu

Portobello Napoleon

GRILLED PORTOBELLO MUSHROOMS, EGGPLANT, RED PEPPERS AND CHEESE

Wine Criteria:

The combination of grilled peppers, eggplant and portobello mushrooms with the goat cheese calls for a medium-bodied, grassy, aromatic white wine such as a California Sauvignon Blanc. Another option is to serve a dry Rosé from the southern regions of France, such as the Rhône Valley or Provence.

Suggestions:

Avignonesi Il Vignola, Tuscany (Italy) **$24**

Sancerre, Loire Valley (France) **$15**

Bernard-Griffin Fumé Blanc, Yakima Valley (Washington State) **$12**

Ferrari Carano Fumé Blanc, Alexander Valley (California) **$12**

Boschendal Estate Sauvignon Blanc, Stellenbosch (South Africa) **$13**

Yarden Sauvignon Blanc, Golan Heights (Israel) **$14**

Château Musar Blanc, Ghazir (Lebanon) **$15**

Tavel Rosé, Rhône Valley (France) **$12**

Fresh Vegetable Pasta
LIGHTLY SAUTÉED GARDEN VEGETABLES IN A LIGHT CREAM SAUCE

Wine Criteria:
Serve a light, unoaked, dry white wine especially those of Northern Italy.

Suggestions:
Est!Est!!Est!!! di Montefiascone, Latium (Italy) **$8**
Friscati, Latium (Italy) **$7**
Vernaccia di San Gimignano, Tuscany (Italy) **$9**
Bianco di Custaza, Veneto (Italy) **$10**
Soave Classico, Veneto (Italy) **$7**
Muscadet de Sevre-et-Maine, Loire Valley (France) **$8**
Vihno Verde, Minho and Douro (Portugal) **$7**
Gruner Veltiner, Lower Austria (Austria) **$13**

Grilled Shrimps with Mustard Sauce
MARINATED IN DIJON MUSTARD AND HONEY

Wine Criteria:
Choose a highly aromatic, fruity or spicy dry white wine with good acidity such as the Riesling and Gewurztraminer from Alsace, France.

Suggestions:
Zemmer Gewurztraminer, Trentino Alto Adige (Italy) **$10**
Weissenkirchener Klaus Riesling, Wachau (Austria) **$20**
Columbia Crest Gewurztraminer, Columbia Valley (Washington State) **$10**
Stone Street Gewurztraminer, Sonoma County (California) **$9**
Riesling, Alsace (France) **$12-$30**
Gewurztraminer, Alsace (France) **$15-$35**

Grilled Banana and Pineapple
TOPPED WITH HONEY, BROWN SUGAR AND NUTS

Wine Criteria:
*Applying the principal of "**contrasting-textures**" can be extremely effective. Since this is a very rich sweet dessert, avoid the "double whammy" and <u>do not</u> choose a very sweet and rich dessert wine, as it could become very cloying. Therefore, I recommend selecting a medium-sweet style white wine from a cool climate that possesses good acidity when it is young such as the Vindage Tardive styles wines from Alsace, France. Or, you could choose a medium-sweet fortified style white wine, such as an Orange Muscat from California.*

Suggestions:
Robert Pecota Moscato di Andrea, Napa (California) **$20**
Quady Essensia, Central Valley (California) **$15**
Valencia Muscatel, Valencia (Spain) **$10-$15**
Moscato D'Asti, Piedmont (Italy) **$13**
Vouvray Demi-Sec, Loire Valley (France) **$7-$11**
Muscat de Beaumes-de-Venise, Rhône Valley (France) **$11 ¹/₂ bt.**
Tokay Pinot Gris "Vendage-Tardive," Alsace (France) **$35-$65**

The Recipes

Portobello Napoleon

Roasted vegetables and cheese make a spectacular presentation when stacked and baked. This dish is guaranteed to impress. (Pictured on our cover.)

Pesto Sauce

1 CUP FRESH BASIL TIGHTLY PACKED, CLEANED AND STEMMED

1 SMALL CLOVE GARLIC

¼ CUP FRESHLY GRATED PARMESAN CHEESE

¼ CUP PINE NUTS

½ TEASPOON SALT

⅓ CUP OLIVE OIL

1 TABLESPOON FRESH LEMON JUICE

In a food processor, put all ingredients except oil, and blend at high speed until mixture is smooth. If necessary, stop machine after first few seconds and scrape down sides of mixing bowl so that all ingredients blend smoothly. Then slowly add oil until you get a smooth consistency. Add additional olive oil if mixture is too thick.

Prepare and Roast Vegetables

1 SMALL EGGPLANT, PEELED AND SLICED ¾" THICK

1 MEDIUM RED PEPPER, ROASTED, PEELED AND SEEDED

2 LARGE PORTOBELLO MUSHROOMS

2 SLICES GOAT CHEESE

1 FRESH MOZZARELLA BALL, CUT INTO 4 SLICES

2 CLOVES GARLIC, CRUSHED

⅓ CUP OLIVE OIL

SALT AND PEPPER TO TASTE

2 LARGE SPRIGS FRESH ROSEMARY (FOR GARNISH)

Preheat broiler. Peel eggplant and slice into ¾" rounds. Salt each slice and let set on cookie sheet for 1 hour, then pat dry with paper towel. In the meantime, roast pepper under broiler until it is charred on all sides. Let cool, peel and seed. Cut into 4 pieces.

Add crushed garlic to oil and let set for at least 15 minutes. Remove stem from portobello mushrooms. Scrape out the black underneath with a small spoon. Brush mushrooms with garlic oil; salt, pepper, then broil or grill for 3 minutes on each side. Set aside until ready to assemble.

After eggplant slices have set for 1 hour, rinse and dry. Lay slices on a baking sheet. Brush both sides with garlic oil, and brown under broiler (or grill) for approximately 7-10 minutes on each side. Eggplant should be golden brown, still firm, but not mushy.

Stack the Napoleon

Preheat oven to 375 degrees F. In a baking dish, make two individual Napoleons by layering roasted vegetables and cheese. Start with an eggplant slice, top with 1 slice roasted red pepper, a slice of fresh mozzarella, a portobello mushroom slice, then another eggplant slice, another slice of roasted red pepper, a slice of goat cheese, placing a small eggplant slice on top. Finish with a slice of fresh mozzarella. Place a toothpick down center to hold everything in a stack. Bake at 375 for 7-10 minutes to heat through.

To serve, place a spoonful of pesto sauce on bottom of two individual plates. Then place the baked Napoleon, and drizzle top with a little more pesto sauce.

Garnish: Replace toothpick with a sprig of rosemary standing up in the middle of Napoleon.

Fresh Vegetable Pasta

*Another colorful and utterly scrumptious pasta dish that is
quick and easy once the vegetables are prepped.*

½ POUND CAPELLINI OR SPAGHETTINI

3 QUARTS WATER

1 TEASPOON SALT

Vegetable Sauce

2 CLOVES GARLIC, MINCED

¼ CUP ONION, DICED

1 SMALL ZUCCHINI, JULIENNED*

1 SMALL STALK CELERY, JULIENNED*

1 LARGE CARROT, JULIENNED*

½ CUP FRESH MUSHROOMS (IN SEASON), SLICED ⅛" THICK

Vegetable Sauce (continued)

1 SMALL RED PEPPER, JULIENNED*

1-16 OUNCE CAN TOMATOES, PEELED AND CHOPPED FINE WITH JUICE

3 TABLESPOONS OLIVE OIL

1 TEASPOON SALT

PEPPER TO TASTE

2 TABLESPOONS FRESH CREAM

2 TABLESPOONS FRESHLY GRATED PARMIGIANO REGGIANO OR PARMESAN CHEESE
(FOR GARNISH)

* Julienne means to cut into short thin strips ¹/₈" across

In a medium skillet, heat oil over medium heat, add garlic and onion. Sauté until golden. Add carrots, celery and salt. Lower heat to medium; cook for 10 minutes. Add red peppers, cook another 5 minutes. Then add zucchini, mushrooms; cook another 10 minutes.

Add tomatoes; cook another 15 minutes. During the last 5 minutes of cooking time, add cream; stir and continue cooking another few minutes.

Bring water to boil, add salt. *Note: Angel hair pasta will cook very quickly, so only cook when you are just about ready to eat.* Add pasta; cook for 5 minutes or until *"al dente."* (Do not over-cook. It is always better to undercook pasta than overcook it.) Drain the pasta; return it to the pan it was cooked in. Gently toss pasta with two-thirds of the vegetables. Reserve some vegetables to garnish the pasta when serving. Serve in pasta bowls.

Garnish: Reserved vegetables and freshly grated Parmigiano Reggiano or parmesan cheese.

Grilled Shrimp with Mustard Sauce

Attention shrimp lovers… this has got to be one of the best recipes you'll ever find for preparing these delectable crustaceans.

12 LARGE UNCOOKED SHRIMP, SHELLED AND DEVEINED, LEAVE TAILS

2 TABLESPOONS OLIVE OIL

1 TABLESPOON DIJON MUSTARD

SALT AND PEPPER TO TASTE

Mix 1 tablespoon of Dijon mustard, 2 tablespoons olive oil, salt and pepper. Toss in shrimp. Let marinate for 30 minutes.

Mustard Sauce

1 TABLESPOON OLIVE OIL

1 LARGE SHALLOTS OR 2 SMALL ONES, CHOPPED FINE

$\frac{1}{8}$ CUP WHITE WINE

3 TABLESPOONS HONEY

1 TABLESPOON DIJON MUSTARD

$\frac{1}{8}$ CUP FRESH LEMON JUICE

3 TABLESPOONS FRESH CREAM

$\frac{1}{2}$ LEMON, SLICED (FOR GARNISH)

2 SPRIGS FRESH ITALIAN PARSLEY (FOR GARNISH)

In small sauce pan, heat oil and sauté shallots until soft. Add wine, simmer until evaporated. Add honey, mustard and lemon juice, let cook for 2 minutes. Add cream at the end. Remove from heat, set aside. Grill shrimp over hot coals for 3-5 minutes. Do not overcook. When done, spoon mustard sauce on the individual plates and place shrimp on top.

Garnish: Fresh lemon slices and sprig of Italian parsley.

Grilled Banana and Pineapple

My favorite desserts are quick, easy and delicious... this one tops the list!

1 BANANA, CUT IN HALF ,THEN CUT LENGTHWISE

2 SLICES PINEAPPLE ROUNDS, CUT 1/2" THICK

1 TABLESPOON BROWN SUGAR

1 TABLESPOON HONEY

2 TABLESPOONS WALNUTS, CHOPPED FINE

1 TABLESPOON BUTTER, CUT IN PIECES

2 SCOOPS VANILLA FROZEN YOGURT

2 FRESH STRAWBERRIES, LEAVE WHOLE WITH STEM AND

1 SPRIG FRESH MINT, FOR GARNISH

Preheat broiler. Cut banana in half, then in half lengthwise. Place on baking sheet and sprinkle with brown sugar, honey, chopped walnuts, and a couple pieces of butter. Cut pineapple in 1/2" rounds. Place on baking sheet with bananas and sprinkle with brown sugar, honey, chopped walnuts, and a couple pieces of butter. Place baking sheet under broiler for 3-5 minutes or until butter melts and tops begin to brown.

Serve on a plate. Arrange pineapple in middle of plate with 2 banana pieces (to the side) pointing away from pineapple round. Place a scoop of vanilla frozen yogurt on top of pineapple.

Garnish: Fresh strawberry and fresh mint sprig

The Menu

Crab Meat Crostini
ITALIAN BREAD TOPPED WITH CRAB MEAT, ONIONS, AND CHEESE

Cannelloni Stuffed with Shrimp, Mushrooms and Ricotta Cheese Filling
STUFFED HOMEMADE PASTA TUBES TOPPED WITH A ROSE CREAM SAUCE

Veal Scaloppini
TOPPED WITH ARTICHOKE HEARTS, SUN-DRIED TOMATOES, MUSHROOMS, CAPERS & BLACK OLIVES

Apple Sachets
PHYLLO DOUGH FILLED WITH APPLES, RICOTTA CHEESE, CINNAMON, NUTS AND GRAND MARNIER

For A Little Romance:

Create a touch of mystery. Leave a message on your lover's voice mail, car seat or in a briefcase. Ask that he come to the front door after work and to ring the bell. Meet him at the door with an apron and a bathing suit underneath. Lead him to the bathroom where another bathing suit is ready for him, along with candles, music, two glasses of wine, and your appetizers. Feed each other while you soak in the bathtub or Jacuzzi (a hot tub or pool will also work). Lead you lover to another room to eat the next course, then finish with dessert in the bedroom. And don't forget the candles, and a glass of bubbly!

Let's Talk Wines For This Menu

Crab Meat Crostini
ITALIAN BREAD TOPPED WITH CRAB MEAT, ONIONS, AND CHEESE

Wine Criteria:
Choose an aromatic, flowery, dry white wine from a cool climate, such as from the region of Alsace in France. These wines retain good acidity which is needed to stand up to the onions in the dish. Or choose a rich, oaky, dry Chardonnay from California with a buttery, silky finish to match the sweet richness of the crab meat. Whatever your choice may be, select a young vintage.

Suggestions:
Riesling, Alsace (France) **$12-$25**
Cloudy Bay Sauvignon Blanc, Marlborough (New Zealand) **$15**
Pouilly Fumé, Loire Valley (France) **$15-$20**
Avignonesi Il Vignole, Tuscany (Italy) **$24**
Sanford "Barrel Select" Chardonnay, Santa Barbara (California) **$35**

Cannelloni
STUFFED WITH SHRIMP, MUSHROOMS, AND RICOTTA CHEESE FILLING

Wine Criteria:
The dominate element is the ricotta cheese, which requires an unoaked, dry, fruity white wine with a high acidity.

Suggestions:
Chablis (young village style) Burgundy (France) **$14-$20**
Montagny 1er Cru, Burgundy (France) **$17**
Muscadet de Sevre-et-Maine, Loire Valley (France) **$8**
R.H. Philips Chardonnay, Central Valley (France) **$8**
Collio Chardonnay, Friuli-Venezia Giulia (Italy) **$15**
Verdicchio, Marches (Italy) **$8-$11**

Veal Scaloppini
TOPPED WITH ARTICHOKE HEARTS, SUN DRIED TOMATOES,
MUSHROOMS, CAPERS AND BLACK OLIVES

Wine Criteria:

Normally I would suggest to serve a rich, buttery, complex white wine, however, this dish is topped with artichokes which is difficult to match with wines. Therefore, you need to choose a very dry white wine with good acidity. To enhance the match further, use the same wine in preparing this dish.

Suggestions:

Chablis (young village style) Burgundy, (France) **$14-$20**
Muscadet de Sevre-et-Maine, Loire Valley, (France) **$8**

If you would like to serve a red wine, choose a light red with high acidity.
Suggestions:

Barbera d'Alba, Piedmont (Italy) **$10-$15**
Cru Beaujolais such as (Moulin-a-Vent Chenas) Burgundy (France) **$11-$14**

Apple Sachets
PHYLLO DOUGH FILLED WITH APPLES, RICOTTA CHEESE, NUTS, AND GRAND MARNIER

Wine Criteria:

Choose a botrytized, sweet white wine such as a Sauternes from Bordeaux, France, or a dry sparkling rosé from California.

Suggestions:

Château Climents, Bordeaux (California) **$35-$65**
Tokaj Aszu "4 Puttonyos", Tokaj-Hegyalia (Hungary) **$15-$20**
Far Niente Dolce, Napa Valley (California) **$16**
Joseph Phelps Delice, Napa Valley (California) **$16**
NV Mumms Cuve Napa Brut Rosé, Napa Valley (California) **$16**

The Recipes

Crab Meat Crostini
A tasty appetizer that takes only minutes… and is a sure winner.

3 OUNCES LUMP CRAB MEAT, FRESH OR CANNED

1/2 SMALL ONION, CHOPPED FINE

2 TABLESPOONS HELLMANS MAYONNAISE

1 OUNCE AMERICAN CHEESE, GRATED FINE

1/2 BAGET FRENCH OR ITALIAN CRUSTY COUNTRY BREAD, SLICED 1/2" THICK

FRESH SPRIG ITALIAN PARSLEY (FOR GARNISH)

Preheat broiler. Cut bread in 1/2" rounds. Clean any bones or shells from crab meat, if using canned. In small bowl, mix crab meat, onions, mayonnaise, grated cheese and blend well. Spread a spoonful of mixture over each bread slice.

Place on a baking sheet, under broiler for a few minutes, until mixture starts to bubble and edges of bread are golden brown.

Garnish: Italian parsley.

Cannelloni Stuffed with Shrimp and Mushrooms

Once the pasta dough is made, these are relatively easy and worth every minute of the time it takes to prepare them. One taste and you'll be a believer.

Homemade Pasta Dough for the Cannelloni

1 CUP UNBLEACHED FLOUR

1 WHOLE EGG

PINCH SALT

Blend egg in a food processor, add salt and flour.

Blend until a ball is formed. Knead and wrap the dough in plastic wrap. Set aside in a cool place for ½ hour to 3 hours. Meanwhile, prepare filling and rosé sauce.

Note: Cannelloni are large pasta squares filled with various fillings and rolled into tubes.

Filling

½ POUND LARGE SHRIMP, PEELED AND DEVEINED

½ CUP FRESH MUSHROOMS, WHITE OR SHITAKE, SLICED

2 TABLESPOONS RICOTTA CHEESE

1 TABLESPOON PARMESAN CHEESE, FRESHLY GRATED

1 WHOLE CLOVE GARLIC

2 TABLESPOONS OLIVE OIL

SALT AND PEPPER, TO TASTE

1 TABLESPOON FRESH ITALIAN PARSLEY, CHOPPED FINE

In a skillet, heat oil and garlic over medium high heat until garlic turns golden. Remove garlic and discard. Raise heat to high; when hot, quickly sauté shrimp about 2-3 minutes. Do not overcook. Remove from pan. Add another tablespoon of oil and heat until hot over high heat. Quickly sauté mushrooms. Remove from heat and drain any excess liquid. On a cutting board combine shrimp and mushrooms, salt and pepper; then chop coarsely. Set aside. Mix ricotta, egg, parmesan cheese and parsley with shrimp and mushroom mixture. Set aside.

Prepare Rosé Sauce
2 TABLESPOONS OLIVE OIL

1 -16 OZ. CAN PLUM TOMATOES, FINELY CHOPPED

1 CLOVE GARLIC, MINCED

6 FRESH BASIL LEAVES, WHOLE

1/2 TEASPOON SALT

PEPPER TO TASTE

3 TABLESPOONS LIGHT CREAM

In a large heavy skillet, sauté garlic until golden. Then add tomatoes, salt, pepper and basil, cook for about 20 minutes. Remove basil leaves. Add light cream the last few minutes of cooking time.

Making and Assembling Cannelloni
3 TABLESPOONS FRESHLY GRATED PARMIGIANO REGGIANO OR PARMESAN CHEESE

FRESH BASIL LEAVES (FOR GARNISH)

When you unwrap the pasta dough, it will seem more moist than it did originally. Do not add any more flour. Dust your hands with flour and knead dough for 1 minute. Divide dough into 2 parts. Flatten each piece, with palm of your hand.

Roll out dough in long strips as wide as possible (about 4" wide) and as thin as possible using a hand-cranked pasta machine. Set rollers of pasta maker at their maximum opening. Run dough through 3 or 4 times, folding and turning it each time you feed it through. Then close the opening one notch, and run dough through once. Continue closing the opening one notch at a time and feed pasta ribbon through the rollers once each time until the lowest notch is reached. **See diagram #3 on page 66.**

Bring 3 quarts of water to a boil. Add salt. Cook pasta strips, 1 at a time, in salted boiling water for 30 seconds to 1 minute. Carefully remove pasta with a large slotted spoon and drop in a bowl of cold water. Quickly remove pasta from cold water and place on a tea towel to drain. Cut pasta strips into 4" X 4" squares.

Preheat oven to 350 degrees F. In a shallow oven proof dish, spread 1/2 of the rosé sauce over bottom of dish. This is where you will put the stuffed cannelloni. Spoon cheese and shrimp mixture the length of each pasta square. Then roll up to make cannelloni tubes. Place cannelloni tubes side by side in the dish, leaving a space between them. Pour more sauce over top, reserving some for garnish. Sprinkle with Parmigiano Reggiano or parmesan cheese. Bake uncovered at 350 degrees F. until bubbly, about 20 minutes.

Garnish: Spoon reserved rosé sauce on plate, placing cannelloni on top with fresh basil leaves.

Diagram #10

Veal Scaloppini with Artichokes and Sun-dried Tomatoes

Unquestionably the most popular of all Italian dishes are those made with veal scaloppini. Here I will share with you the secrets for preparing the most tender veal scaloppini ever!

4 SLICES VEAL SCALOPPINI*

2 TABLESPOONS FLOUR

SALT AND PEPPER TO TASTE

3 TABLESPOONS OLIVE OIL

1 WHOLE CLOVE GARLIC

6 ARTICHOKES HEARTS PACKED IN OIL, DRAINED AND CHOPPED

6 SUN-DRIED TOMATOES, PACKED IN OIL, SLICED

1 TABLESPOON CAPERS

1 TABLESPOON BLACK OLIVES, GREEK OR ITALIAN, PITTED AND CHOPPED

5 FRESH WHITE MUSHROOMS, SLICED

1 MEDIUM FRESH TOMATO, DICED

* *The secret is the right cut of veal. The butcher must use the top round of veal in one solid piece and cut it against the grain to make the scaloppini. Unless they are cut this way, the scaloppini will toughen, shrink and curl when cooked. The scaloppini must be pounded to a very thin consistency which also contributes to the delicacy of the dish.*

Drain artichoke hearts. Slice sun-dried tomatoes. Clean and slice mushrooms, dice tomato. Pit and slice black olives. Mix all ingredients and salt lightly. Marinate for 1/2 hour to 1 hour. Then sauté mixture for several minutes. Salt and pepper to taste, and set aside.

Place veal slices in a plastic bag and pound very thin with the flat side of a meat cleaver. *The proper pounding procedure is to bring the meat cleaver down on the center of the meat and slide from the center outward in one continuous motion. Do this until each scaloppini is thinned out evenly.* Salt and pepper both sides of veal, then flour generously.

Heat oil and garlic in large frying pan, until garlic turns golden brown. Remove garlic and discard. Turn heat to high and when hot, quickly sauté veal slices, approximately 45 seconds per side. Add wine, cook until it evaporates. Remove from heat and add lemon juice. Serve on individual plates.

Garnish: Sautéed vegetables.

Apple Sachets

They are light, crisp and a winner for cooks who are not fancy bakers.
These little sachets look and taste delicious!

6 SHEETS PHYLLO DOUGH CUT TO 6″ X 6″ PIECES

2 TABLESPOONS BUTTER

2 SMALL APPLES, CORED, PEELED AND CHOPPED

1 TABLESPOON BROWN SUGAR

DASH GRAND MARNIER OR TRIPLE SEC

¼ CUP RICOTTA CHEESE

PINCH CINNAMON

3 TABLESPOONS HAZELNUTS OR WALNUTS

OPTIONAL: 1 TEASPOON WHITE RAISINS

2 TEASPOONS POWDERED SUGAR (FOR GARNISH)

1 OUNCE MELTED CHOCOLATE (FOR GARNISH)

Preheat oven to 375 degrees F. Peel, core and chop apples in small pieces. In a small saucepan add butter, liqueur, apples, optional raisins, and cook until apples are tender, approximately 10 minutes. Remove from heat and let cool. In a small bowl, combine ricotta cheese with apple mixture. Sprinkle mixture with cinnamon and roasted nuts. Set aside. Lay 2 sheets of phyllo dough out flat, brush each sheet lightly with melted butter around edges. Place 2 tablespoons of apple mixture in center of dough; leave 2" border on all sides. Pull sides up and tie loosely with a string to make a sachet. Repeat for other sachet. Place apple sachets on a greased baking sheet, drizzle tops with melted butter. Bake at 375 degrees F for 15-20 minutes or until golden brown. Remove string and serve.

Garnish: Powdered sugar and/or melted chocolate.

Caprese Salad
FRESH TOMATOES, MOZZARELLA AND BASIL

Asparagus Risotto
ITALIAN ARBORIO RICE WITH ASPARAGUS AND FRESH PARMESAN CHEESE

Chicken Parmesan
BREADED CHICKEN BREASTS BAKED WITH GRILLED EGGPLANT, CHEESE AND TOMATO SAUCE

Italian Waffle Baskets
FILLED WITH VANILLA YOGURT AND TOPPED FRESH RASPBERRY SAUCE

For A Little Romance:

Purchase a crown at a novelty store, or make one large enough to fit your lover's head. Place it on the dinner table next to his/her plate with a note that reads: Tonight is your night…you're "King/Queen for the Night" and the entire evening will be devoted to your pleasures. YES!!

The secret to remember with all these romantic ideas is you've got to be adventurous, as well as creative, as you make the necessary preparations for dinner and romance. These romantic ideas are just that… add, delete, or combine them in a way that you are comfortable. Buon Appetito, and may everyday of your life be filled with good food, wine and ROMANCE!

Let's Talk Wines For This Menu

Caprese Salad
FRESH TOMATOES, MOZZARELLA AND BASIL

Wine Criteria:
Choose a dry rosé wine or a dry sparkling rosé, the drier the better. (An enchanting way to start an evening.)

Suggestions:
Tavel Rosé, Rhône Valley (France) **$12**
Sancerre Rosé, Loire Valley (France) **$15**
Mumms Cuvée Napa Brut Rosé, Napa (California) **$16**
Vintage Iron Horse Brute Rosé, Sonoma (California) **$24**
Bollinger Grand Anne Brut Rosé, Champagne (France) **$100**

Asparagus Risotto
ITALIAN ARBORIO RICE WITH ASPARAGUS AND FRESH PARMESAN CHEESE

Wiue Criteria:
Asparagus is another item that is difficult to match with wine, as it makes most wines taste metallic. Therefore, choose a simple unoaked, dry white wine. The idea is to select a wine that the asparagus can inflict little or no damage on.

Suggestions:
Est! Est!! Est!!! di Montefiascone DOC, Latium (Italy) **$10**
Il Taso Orvieto Classico, Veneto (Italy) **$8**
Soave Classico, Veneto (Italy) **$5-$8**
Verdicchio, Marches (Italy) **$12**
Muscadet de Sevre-et-Maine, Loire Valley (France) **$8**
Vinho Verde DOC, Minho (Portugal) **$7**

Chicken Parmesan

BREADED CHICKEN BREASTS BAKED WITH GRILLED EGGPLANT, CHEESE AND TOMATO SAUCE

Wine Criteria:

In this dish you need to choose a wine to match the smoky bitterness of the eggplant, and the acidity of the tomato sauce. Therefore select a dry rosé or a grassy, fruity white wine with fairly good acidity.

Suggestions:

Tavel Rosé, Rhône Valley (France) **$13**
Pouilly-Fumé, Loire Valley (France) **$15-$20**
Murphy-Goode Fumé Blanc, Alexander Valley (California) **$12**

Or you may serve a medium-bodied, dry red wine that is packed with spicy fruits.

Suggestions:

Côtes du Rhône Village, Rhône Valley (France) **$10**
Backsberg Pinotage, Paarl Wo (South Africa) **$12**
Rosemount Estate Shiraz, New South Wales (Australia) **$10**
Cakebread Zinfandel, Napa Valley (California) **$15**
Salice Salentino Riserva DOC, Apulia (Italy) **$10**

Italian Waffle Baskets

FILLED WITH VANILLA YOGURT, TOPPED WITH RASPBERRY SAUCE

Wine Criteria:

The acidity in the fresh raspberry sauce will not do many dessert wines any favor, except those with high acidity, such as Sauternes from France. Therefore choose the previously described wine or a delicate, dry style Champagne or sparkling wine in the Blanc de Blancs style (i.e., made from Chardonnay grapes only).

Suggestions:

Sauternes, such as Château Climent, Bordeaux (France) **$30-$60**
Cristal Blanc de Blancs, Champagne (France) **$150**
Scharffenberger Blanc de Blancs, Mendocino County (California) **$20**
Brachetta D'Acqui, Piedmont (Italy) **$14**

The Recipes

Caprese Salad

A classic Italian salad that takes only minutes to prepare, made with
fresh tomatoes, fresh mozzarella and fresh basil.

2 MEDIUM RIPE FRESH PLUM TOMATOES, SLICED INTO 8 SLICES

1 LARGE FRESH MOZZARELLA BALL, SLICED INTO 8 THIN SLICES

8 FRESH BASIL LEAVES, CHOPPED

SALT AND PEPPER, TO TASTE

2 TABLESPOONS OLIVE OIL

Wash and dry tomatoes. *Only use red and ripe tomatoes for this recipe.* Slice tomatoes into eight ¼" slices. Salt and set aside. Slice fresh mozzarella ball, into eight thin slices. Rinse and dry fresh basil leaves. Arrange on two individual plates, alternating cheese and tomato slices and a piece of fresh basil leaf. Drizzle with olive oil, salt and pepper.

Asparagus Risotto

Risotto must be made with Italian arborio rice which is thicker and shorter
than our well known long-grain rice. When cooked slowly in broth it has an
unusual creamy texture that is truly unique.

¾ CUP ARBORIO RICE

½ CUP WHITE WINE

1 WHOLE CLOVE GARLIC

3 SHALLOTS, CHOPPED

8 ASPARAGUS SPEARS, COOKED & CHOPPED

3 CUPS CHICKEN STOCK

1 OUNCE PROSCIUTTO COTTO* CHOPPED FINE

3 TABLESPOONS FRESHLY GRATED PARMESAN CHEESE

1/2 TEASPOON SALT

PEPPER TO TASTE

* *Proscuitto Cotto is Italian cooked ham, available at Italian specialty stores*

Bring 3-4 cups of water to boil. Add salt. Add asparagus to boiling water and cook over medium heat for 5 minutes. Remove several bright green spears and set aside for garnish. Continue cooking the remaining asparagus for another 5-10 minutes until soft. Strain asparagus, reserving 1 cup cooking water from asparagus for later. Chop asparagus and set aside.

In a medium size pan, heat chicken stock until hot. Leave on low. Meanwhile, in a heavy skillet heat oil until hot. Sauté the shallots, garlic, proscuitto for 3-5 minutes. Add wine and let evaporate. Then add rice and cook for 5 minutes, stirring constantly. Add salt and asparagus. Add enough chicken stock to cover rice (1/2 cup at a time). Stir thoroughly. When rice absorbs most of stock, add more stock and stir again. This will take 20-30 minutes. *Note: If you run out of chicken stock, use reserved water asparagus was cooked in.* Rice is done when it is firm, but not raw in center. Stir in half of parmesan cheese and dish up.

Garnish: Reserved parmesan cheese and blanched asparagus.

Chicken Parmesan with Eggplant

A variation of the traditional eggplant parmesan, whereby we have added sautéed chicken breasts, making a hearty and delicious entrée.

Prepare the Eggplant

1 SMALL EGGPLANT (ABOUT 3/4 LB.), PEELED AND SLICED INTO 3/4 INCH SLICES

2 TABLESPOONS OLIVE OIL

SALT TO TASTE

Partially peel skin of eggplant with a vegetable peeler lengthwise, leaving a strip of skin every other inch. Slice in 3/4" slices. *Be careful not to slice eggplant slices too thin.* Salt, and let set for 1 hour. (This allows some of the bitter juices to seep out.) After 1 hour, blot eggplant with a paper towel. Oil a baking sheet and brush both sides of eggplant with oil. Arrange in a single layer on baking sheet and broil for about 5-7 minutes on each side or until golden brown. *The eggplant should be golden but not mushy.*

Prepare the Chicken Breasts

2 WHOLE CHICKEN BREASTS (BONED AND SKINLESS)

1/2 CUP UNSEASONED BREAD CRUMBS

3 TABLESPOONS FLOUR

1 WHOLE EGG, BEATEN WITH 1 TABLESPOON MILK

2 WHOLE CLOVES GARLIC

SALT AND PEPPER TO TASTE

1 LARGE FRESH MOZZARELLA BALL, SLICED INTO 1/4" THICK SLICES

1/4 CUP FRESHLY GRATED PARMIGIANO REGGIANO OR PARMESAN

4 TABLESPOONS OLIVE OIL

Cut chicken breasts in half. Place chicken breasts in a plastic bag (or between two sheets of plastic wrap) and pound until 1/4 inch thick with smooth side of a meat mallet.

Salt and pepper both sides. Dip in flour, then egg wash, then bread crumbs. In a large frying pan, heat remaining 2 tablespoons olive oil and garlic over medium heat until golden. Remove garlic and turn up heat. Sauté breaded chicken breasts until golden brown on both sides. *Try using a splatter screen when you are cooking the chicken at such a high temperature.*

Prepare Tomato Sauce

3 TABLESPOONS OLIVE OIL

1 CLOVE FRESH GARLIC, MINCED

1- 8 OZ. CAN ITALIAN PLUM TOMATOES, CHOPPED

8 LEAVES FRESH BASIL

1/2 TEASPOON SALT

PEPPER TO TASTE

In a skillet, heat oil and garlic over medium high heat garlic turns until golden. Add chopped tomatoes, salt and pepper and 4 of the basil leaves. Simmer for 20 minutes. Reserve remaining basil leaves for garnish.

To Assemble Chicken Parmesan in a Baking Dish

Preheat oven to 350 degrees F. Place chicken breasts on bottom of an oblong baking dish. Place eggplant slices on top of chicken breasts. Sprinkle with grated Parmigiano Reggiano cheese followed by fresh mozzarella slices. Bake in oven until cheese melts, about 15 minutes.

Garnish: Spoon a generous amount of tomato sauce onto individual plates. Place chicken parmesan on top of sauce, then spoon additional sauce over top adding a few fresh basil leaves.

Italian Waffle Baskets with Frozen Yogurt and Berries
(pictured on the cover)

Depending on how much time you have, you can buy or make these waffle baskets a.k.a. "Pizelle" which is an Italian word meaning "charming little pizzas." These crisp anise wafer scented cookies are made using a special non-stick iron and formed into baskets while they are still warm.

2 ITALIAN PIZELLE WAFFLE BASKETS, STORE-BOUGHT OR HOMEMADE

To make the homemade Italian waffle baskets you will need an Italian Pizelle Maker, which is similar to a Belgian Waffle Maker, but the shape is round and the waffle is wafer thin.

Homemade Pizelle
2 WHOLE EGGS

¼ CUP CANOLA OR MAZOLA OIL

⅓ CUP SUGAR

½ TEASPOON BAKING POWDER

¾ CUP FLOUR

1 TEASPOON VANILLA EXTRACT

1-3 DROPS ANISE OIL

This recipe yields 14 pizelle, make 2 baskets and leave the remainder flat. Store in a plastic bag. They are delicious as cookies.

Sift flour and baking powder in a mixing bowl. In another bowl, beat eggs and sugar together, then add the oil, vanilla and (optional) anise oil and beat until blended. Add flour to the egg mixture and stir until blended. Preheat the Italian Pizelle Maker. Lightly oil or coat the inside of the pizelle maker with nonstick cooking spray. Using a tablespoon scoop up enough of the batter to fill the spoon. Use another spoon to push the batter onto the center of the iron. Close the iron and squeeze it to evenly distribute the batter. Bake until golden brown, about 30 seconds to 1 minute.

Remove pizelle from the maker with a metal spatula, and immediately, while still hot, place it over bottom of a small drinking glass and shape into a basket. You must do this quickly. So get the glass and have it close by before making them. Use care since basket will be fragile. Let cool.

Topping
1 CUP FRESH RASPBERRIES

1/4 CUP SUGAR

2 TABLESPOON FRESH LEMON JUICE

1/4 CUP FRESH BLUEBERRIES

1/4 CUP FRESH STRAWBERRIES, SLICED THIN
OR WHATEVER BERRIES ARE IN SEASON AND LOOK GOOD

1 PINT FROZEN VANILLA YOGURT OR ICE CREAM

CHOCOLATE SAUCE AND CONFECTIONERS SUGAR (FOR GARNISH)

Raspberry Sauce
1 CUP FRESH RASPBERRIES

1/4 CUP SUGAR

1/4 CUP SPARKING WHITE WINE OR CHAMPAGNE

Rinse 1 cup of fresh raspberries in cold water. In small saucepan, put raspberries and sugar, and sparkling white wine; stir and bring to boil. Turn heat down and simmer for 10 minutes. Strain berries through a mesh strainer over a bowl, reserving raspberry sauce.

Serve on individual serving plates. Spoon raspberry sauce on plate. Place waffle basket on top. Fill each waffle basket with a scoop of frozen yogurt and sprinkle with mixed fruit.

Garnish: Melted chocolate sauce and/or confectioners sugar.

$\mathcal{T}$HE WINE GLOSSARY

ACIDITY: Refers to the pH level of young wines produced from grapes grown in cooler climates. Such wines possess high levels of acidity and tend to feel astringent or austere on the palate. Wines that possess good fruits balanced with good acidity make your mouth pucker and stand up to the notes of their lively fruits. In this case, the wine can be described as being complemented with refreshing acidity.

AROMATIC: A tasting term that describes the fresh and fruity smells reminiscent of some white wines. These qualities are usually more apparent in wines made from the Riesling, Gewurztraminer, and Sauvignon Blanc grapes, especially when grown in cooler climates.

BOTRYTISED: Refers to certain wines produced from grapes affected by botrytis, which is a form of rot called "noble rot" by wine makers. When the botrytis forms on the grapes, it absorbs the water thus increasing its sugar content. The grapes then shrivel and intensify in flavor. Wines produced from these grapes are usually sweet, rich, and possess a honey-like flavor.

CLOYING: A term used to describe wines that are too sweet without having a compensating acidity. This term also refers to the taste combination of food and wine together that is described as sickly sweet or heavy.

CREMANT: Originally, a term used to describe sparkling wine with gentler, softer bubbles than Champagne. Today Cremant refers to sparkling wines from the Appellations of Cremant de Bourgogne located in the northern part of the Burgundy region in France.

CRISP: A term used to describe wines with good refreshing acidity.

ELEGANT: A tasters term used to describe a wine that possesses the qualities of refinement. These qualities include, but are not necessarily limited only to, good balance, intense flavor, smooth texture, and long finish. On the other hand, this term is used to describe balanced and delicate Champagnes.

FLOWERY: A term commonly used to describe the aroma of some young white wines. These wines are usually produced from grapes grown in cooler climates such as, Riesling grown in the Alsace region of France, or in the Mosel region of Germany.

FORTIFIED WINES: Wines whose natural strength is increased with added alcohol, either during fermentation to preserve the natural sweetness (as in Port) or after they have fermented to dryness (as in Sherry.)

GRASSY: A tasting term used to describe herbaceous wines, usually the characteristic of the Sauvignon Blanc grape. The aroma of such wines resembles that of fresh cut grass.

ICE STYLE WINES (EISWEIN): A German wine making concept, whereby the botrytized grapes are picked and crushed early in the morning when they are still frozen by frost or snow. The Ice style process allows the producer to extract pure juice thus leaving the water behind in the form of ice. However, some wine makers in California produce Ice style wines by freezing the grapes themselves before crushing.

LEES: Dead yeast cells that are usually left in the cask during fermentation. Some wines are kept on their lees for an extended period. This enables the wine to undergo chemical changes that increase the wine's flavor and complexity. A wine described on the label as "sur lie" has been kept in contact with its lees until bottling. These wines are known to have an effervescent or slight bubbly character.

LIGHT-BODIED, MEDIUM-BODIED, FULL-BODIED: Refers to the weight of the wine and the way it feels in the mouth. Light-bodied wines feel thin, while full-bodied wines feel robust and chewy.

MINERALY: A tasting term used to describe the steely or mineraly aftertaste on the finish of some wines. A couple examples of this would be a Chablis from Burgundy, France, or a Vinho Verde from Spain. In food, briny oysters can be described as mineraly.

OAKY: A term that describes the woody after taste which is a result of fermenting and/or aging the wine in oak barrels.

ROMANTIC WINE MATCH: The symbol of a heart "❤" will appear before some wine selections. This heart indicates a wine match that would be appropriate to serve for more than one course.

SPICY: A tasting term used to describe the spicy wine flavors of cloves, cinnamon, and nutmeg. Examples would be some young California Cabernets and Zinfandels, as well as some barrel fermented Chardonnays, and Gewurztraminer.

TANNIN: A natural compound found only in red wines as a result of crushing the grapes with their skin, stems, and pips, then aged in wood barrels. Wines with a high level of tannins (especially young red wines) tend to have an astringent and abrasive scrape on the gums, tongue, and teeth, much like the feel in your mouth when drinking a very strong tea, or eating a potato skin. Tannin is an important element to consider in food and wine matching as it cuts through the fattiness of meats and cheeses. It also acts as a preservative while the wine is aging.

UNOAKED: Wines that are not exposed to oak. Such wines are fermented in stainless steel tanks rather than oak barrels. These wines possess crisp clean fruit flavors, and they tend to be light to medium-bodied.

VISCOUS: A term used to describe the thickness and richness of some wines. It is directly related to what tasters call body (see the term Full-Bodied). Wines with high viscosity tend to look somewhat foggy in the glass. Viscosity comes from high levels of glycerin, alcohol, and sugar in the wine. Therefore, the most viscous wines are those of high alcohol strength and sugar content, such as very sweet dessert wines.

VINTAGE PORT OR VINTAGE CHARACTER PORT: A Port wine that is aged for two years in a wood cask, then matured (aged) in the bottle. It is usually sweeter than the Tawny Port, which is matured (aged) in a wood cask until it's bottled.

Bibliography

Lorenza De'Medici, *The Heritage of Italian Cooking*. New York: Random House 1990

Alexandra Stoddard, *Living a Beautiful Life*. New York: Avon Books 1986

Godek, Gregory J.P., *1001 Ways To Be Romantic*. Massachusetts: Casablanca Press, Inc. 1993

Marcella Hazan, *Essentials of Classic Italian Cooking*. New York: Alfred A. Knopf, 1992

Harriet Lembeck, 7th Edition, *Grossman's Guide to Wines, Beers, and Spirits*. New York: Charles Scribner's and Son's 1983

David Rosengarten and Jashua Wesson, *Red Wine with Fish*. New York: Simon and Schuster 1989

Jancis Robinson, *Master of Wine The Oxford Companion to Wine*. Oxford New York: Oxford University Press, 1994

Tom Stevenson, Master of Wine, *Sotheby's World Wine Encyclopedia*. London: Dorling Kindersley Limited, 1988

Oz Clarke, *Pocket Wine Guide*. England: Webster's International Publishers 1993-1996

Index

Anchovy and Black Olive
Crostini, ... 84

APPETIZERS
Anchovy and Black Olive
Crostini, ... 84
Bruschetta with Roasted
Peppers, ... 128
Caesar Salad, ... 73
Caprese Salad, ... 158
Crabmeat Crostini, ... 148
Eggplant Roll-Ups, ... 106
Fried Baby Artichokes, . . . 119
Mozzarella Balls with
Pesto, ... 95
Pizza Capricciosa, ... 62
Portobello Napoleon, ... 139
Seafood Fritters, ... 54
Zucchini Cakes, ... 41
Apple Sachets, ... 154
Artichokes, Fried Baby, . . . 119
Asparagus Risotto, ... 158

Banana Pineapple with
Honey and Nuts 144
Bite-sized Cream Puffs, ... 57
Bruschetta with Roasted
Peppers. 128

Caesar Salad 73
Cannelloni with Shrimps
and Mushrooms, ... 149

Cannoli, Normals, ... 111
Caprese Salad 158

CHICKEN
Chicken Breasts with
Rosemary, ... 100
Chicken Florentine, ... 131
Chicken Parmesan, ... 160
Chicken Saltimbocca, ... 45
Crabmeat Crostini, ... 148

DESSERTS
Apple Sachets, ... 154
Bite-size Cream Puffs, ... 57
Espresso Granita, ... 124
Fresh Berries and
Frozen Yogurt, ... 47
Grilled Bananas and
Pineapple, ... 144
Italian Kisses, ... 133
Italian Waffle Baskets
fill with Fruit, ... 162
Macedonia, ... 90
Norma's Cannoli. 111
Stuffed Apple Wrapped
in Phyllo, ... 77
Tiramisù, ... 68
Zuccotto alla Ricotta, ... 101

Espresso Granita, ... 124
Eggplant Roll-Ups, ... 106

FISH AND SHELLFISH
Cannelloni with Shrimp
and Mushrooms 149
Crabmeat Crostini, ... 148
Grilled Shrimp, ... 143

Seafood Fettuccine, ... 85
Seafood Fritters, ... 54
Seared Salmon, ... 67
Spaghettini with
Tuna, ... 55
Tilapia Pizzaiola, ... 110
Fried Baby Artichokes, ... 119
Fresh Vegetable Pasta, ... 141

Grilled Bananas and
Pineapple, ... 144
Grilled Lamb Chops
with Rosemary, ... 76
Grilled Shrimp, ... 143
Grilled Veal Chops, ... 123
Gnocchi, Ricotta with
Bolognese Sauce, ... 42

Homemade Croutons 74

Italian Kisses 133
Italian Waffle Baskets 162

Lamb Chops, Grilled, ... 76
Lasagna, Vegetable, ... 96

Marinara Sauce 108
Macedonia, ... 90
Mozzarella Balls
with Pesto, ... 95

PASTA AND RICE
Asparagus Risotto, ... 158
Cannelloni Stuffed
with Shrimp and
Mushrooms, ... 149
Fresh Vegetable Pasta . . . 141

Pasta with Zucchini and
   Shitake Mushrooms, . . . 75
Ricotta Agnolotti, ... 64
Ricotta Gnocchi
   Bolognese, ... 42
Seafood Fettuccine, ... 121
Seafood Ravioli, ... 85
Spaghettini Marinara, . . . 108
Spaghetti and
   Meatballs, ... 129
Spaghettini with
   Tuna, ... 55
Vegetable Lasagna, ... 96
Pizza Capricciosa, ... 62
Pizelle, Homemade, ... 162
Portobello Napoleon, ... 139

Raspberry Sauce 163
Ravioli, Seafood, ... 85
Red Pepper Sauce 86
Ricotta Agnolotti, ... 64
Ricotta Gnocchi, ... 42
Risotto, Asparagus, ... 158
Rose Sauce, ... 150

Seafood Fritters 154
Seafood Fettuccine, ... 121
Seafood Ravioli, ... 85
Seared Salmon, ... 67
Spaghettini Marinara, ... 108
Spaghetti and
   Meatballs, ... 129
Spaghettini with Tuna, ... 55

Stuffed Apples Wrapped
   in Phyllo, ... 77

Tilapia Pizzaiola, ... 110
Tiramisù 68

VEAL
Veal Chops, Grilled,
   with Wild
   Mushrooms 123
Veal Milanese, ... 88
Veal Scaloppini with
   Fresh Sage, ... 56
Veal Scaloppini with
   Artichokes and
   Sundried Tomatoes, . . . 152
Vegetable Lasagna, ... 96

Zucchini Cakes, ... 41
Zuccotta alla Ricotta, ... 101

Additional Information

If you are unable to obtain a copy of *Romance Begins In The Kitchen* from your local bookstore, you may send $14.95 (plus $3.50 shipping and handling) to:

Romance Begins in the Kitchen
c/o Bause House Publications
P.O. Box 147
Union Lake, MI 48387-0147

For fastest delivery or credit card orders call or fax your order today.

Telephone: (248) 366-0590 (Bause House Publications)
 (248) 816-5000 (Sommelier Connections)
Fax: (248) 363-8080
Website: www.bausehouse.com

Or fill out this form and mail it along with a check or money order to the address listed above.

_____ Books @ $14.95 each .... $_____
Shipping $3.50 for the 1st book.................. $_____
Plus $1.50 for each additional book............ $_____
Michigan Residents please add 6% tax......... $_____
 TOTAL............ $_____

Name _____   ☐ VISA   ☐ Mastercard

Company _____   Credit Card Account # _____

Address_____   Expiration Date_____

City _____ State __ Zip _____   Authorized Signature_____

Phone _____

ROMANCE BEGINS
IN THE KITCHEN

Cover Design by Barbara Hodge

Text Design by Barbara Hodge in
Adobe Garamond, Univers 45 Light and
65 Bold, Vivaldi, and Sloop Script Two

Text Stock is 60 lb. Windsor Smooth

Printed and bound by McNaughton & Gunn
Saline, Michigan

Production Editor: Alex Moore